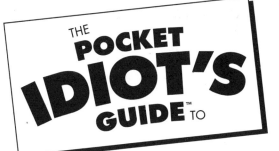

THE POCKET IDIOT'S GUIDE TO

Family Reunions

394.2 Z19
Zavatta, Amy.
The pocket idiot's guide to
family reunions

by Amy Zavatto

MID-CONTINENT PUBLIC LIBRARY
Colbern Road Branch
1000 N.E. Colbern Road
Lee's Summit, Mo. 64C

D1564671

ALPHA

A Pearson Education Company

Copyright © 2002 by Pearson Education, Inc.

All rights reserved. No part of this book shall be reproduced, stored in a retrieval system, or transmitted by any means, electronic, mechanical, photocopying, recording, or otherwise, without written permission from the publisher. No patent liability is assumed with respect to the use of the information contained herein. Although every precaution has been taken in the preparation of this book, the publisher and author assume no responsibility for errors or omissions. Neither is any liability assumed for damages resulting from the use of information contained herein. For information, address Alpha Books, 201 West 103rd Street, Indianapolis, IN 46290.

THE POCKET IDIOT'S GUIDE TO and Design are registered trademarks of Pearson Education, Inc.

International Standard Book Number: 0-02-864388-7
Library of Congress Catalog Card Number: 2002103796

04   03   02   8   7   6   5   4   3   2   1

Interpretation of the printing code: The rightmost number of the first series of numbers is the year of the book's printing; the rightmost number of the second series of numbers is the number of the book's printing. For example, a printing code of 02-1 shows that the first printing occurred in 2002.

Printed in the United States of America

Note: This publication contains the opinions and ideas of its author. It is intended to provide helpful and informative material on the subject matter covered. It is sold with the understanding that the author and publisher are not engaged in rendering professional services in the book. If the reader requires personal assistance or advice, a competent professional should be consulted.

The author and publisher specifically disclaim any responsibility for any liability, loss, or risk, personal or otherwise, which is incurred as a consequence, directly or indirectly, of the use and application of any of the contents of this book.

For marketing and publicity, please call: 317-581-3722

The publisher offers discounts on this book when ordered in quantity for bulk purchases and special sales.

For sales within the United States, please contact: Corporate and Government Sales, 1-800-382-3419 or corpsales@pearsontechgroup.com

Outside the United States, please contact: International Sales, 317-581-3793 or international@pearsontechgroup.com

To my husband, Dan Marotta, for always supporting me and my five million moods.

To my phenomenal, gorgeous sisters, Linda, Janet, and Laura, who continually show me that family is a source for really good jokes.

To my father, Michael Zavatto, for teaching me not to be lazy and that anything can be accomplished as long as you keep at it.

To my beautiful, beautiful mother, sweet Virginia Zavatto, for things too innumerable to count, but also for being the family glue—a job she made look effortless, but was a lot harder than it looked. We miss you every day.

MID-CONTINENT PUBLIC LIBRARY

3 0002 00101483 6

MID-CONTINENT PUBLIC LIBRARY
Colbern Road Branch
1000 N.E. Colbern Road
Lee's Summit, Mo. 64086

CR

Contents

Appendixes

Introduction

We've all heard the words attributed to Ben Franklin: In this world nothing is certain but death and taxes. Ah, but old Ben overlooked one other very important constant in life that is (well, most of the time) a decidedly happier given: family. We've all got one. Some are of the traditional, nuclear type and traceable back to ye olde *Mayflower*, and some are so chock full of in-laws, out-laws, and steps that they truly resemble a melting pot. Whatever the make-up of your kooky, beautiful clan, they're your history, your blood, your friends, your mirror. In many ways, they even define who you are and who you've become.

When I was 13, my mother's cousin Winifred organized a reunion at her home in Lido Beach, Long Island, for the Irish side of the family. At that point, I only knew I had a grandmother, grandfather, one uncle, one aunt, and two cousins from my mother's side. When my mother and I showed up to the all-day affair, my jaw dropped. There were *hundreds* of relatives! I met second cousins, third cousins, first cousins once removed. The ages spanned from kids younger than me to my cousin Joe, a dapper man in his 90s who told me such wonderful stories about our family's adventures in County Longford that I was completely enraptured (and forgot all about the day-long Jerry Lewis movie-a-thon that I was missing that day). I had fun, I made new friends with cousins I'd never known existed before that day, and I learned about my heritage. Most important, though, I felt a part of something unique and very special: my family.

Maybe you've been to a family reunion and loved the experience. Maybe you feel a Christmas card once a year just isn't good enough and want to pull in the wagons a bit. Whatever your reason, a family reunion is a wonderful way to bring together these people who, for better or worse, are part of your past, your present, and your future.

What's Inside

This little book will help you—the designated torch carrier of family fun—to plan a bang-up reunion that will be forever remembered in the annals of family lore (and which may even become a new family tradition for years to come). You'll find all the ingredients for planning a fab family fandango here—from creating a guest list to tracing your roots to smoothing over family squabbles to planning some great reunion fun and games. That's what makes *The Pocket Idiot's Guide to Family Reunions* indispensable in your quest to create an event to remember. It leaves no stone unturned—from very practical advice to tips on dealing with those more delicate, sticky family situations. You'll learn how to keep it all organized and remain on top of the planning from beginning to end.

Along the way you'll find the following extras in this book:

Clan Clues _____

Check these boxes for valuable bits of information and tips to ensure that your reunion planning is as smooth as Aunt Greta's famous homemade chocolate pudding.

Say Uncle! _____

No party plan can go completely without a hitch. These boxes point out possible pitfalls to avoid so you can steer clear of any reunion-related rigmarole.

Family Jewels _____

These boxes contain fun quotes from some famous folks on the affair known as family.

Acknowledgments

Thanks to …

Randy Ladenheim-Gil, my former editorial partner in crime, who always keeps me laughing and looking at the bright side. Marie Butler-Knight, for giving me the green light. Development editor Lynn Northrup, because there's nothing better than working with a real pro. Senior production editor Christy Wagner, for doing the thankless hard stuff and always being cheery about it. Phil Kitchel, for his patience, past and present, with all my dopey questions and whining.

The Zavatto clan—from the East Coast (hi, Aunt I!) to the West Coast (Susan, you're still the coolest)—we're very lucky to have each other. As families go, you're all aces. Wilma Runyon and the Marotta family, for showing me that family doesn't necessarily have to be blood-related. Bonnie Burrell, for her help as a reunion veteran. Patricia McNally, for kicking my butt way back when and being the best teacher a kid could hope to have.

Trademarks

All terms mentioned in this book that are known to be or are suspected of being trademarks or service marks have been appropriately capitalized. Alpha Books and Pearson Education, Inc., cannot attest to the accuracy of this information. Use of a term in this book should not be regarded as affecting the validity of any trademark or service mark.

A Reunion by Any Other Name

In This Chapter

- What kind of reunion should you throw?
- Make a party on your patio
- Take your outing off-site
- Have a whirlwind weekend of family fun

You've got your address book out. Your hand is poised on the telephone receiver to start rounding up the relatives for a get-together you'll be talking about for years to come. But hold on there, kin corral-er. You have to answer a very important question first: What kind of reunion do you want (and are you prepared) to have?

Well, you ask, what's to decide? We'll all just get together and that will be that. Ah, but it's not that simple. Think, for example, about an occasion when you've organized a dinner party. You thought about how many people you wanted to invite, how many could fit in the space you have, how formal or informal you wanted it to be, how much food you needed to buy, what time you wanted your guests to show up (and leave), and a host of other details to ensure a pleasant evening for all. It's the same with a reunion.

Before you get on the horn and start rounding up the troops, you need to decide what kind of reunion you want to have. In this chapter, we'll look at several basic reunion types to help you figure out which best suits your clan and your plan.

Family Jewels

The family—that dear octopus from whose tentacles we never quite escape, nor, in our inmost hearts, ever quite wish to.

—Dodie Smith, author of *101 Dalmatians* (1938)

Pick a Party

The first thing you need to do before you start thinking about "who" is deciding "what." In other words, what kind of party are you going to plan? We can break down the reunion scheme into a few basic types:

- An informal afternoon gathering at home (approximately 10 to 50 people; 3 to 6 months of planning time)

- A larger gathering at a rented spot (approximately 50 to 100 people; 6 months to 1 year of planning time)
- A weekend-long family extravaganza (approximately 100 to 200 people; 1 to $1^1/_2$ years of planning time)

Within these basic parameters you can decide many other things, such as theme and reason for the gathering (an anniversary or birthday, for example), how formal or informal you want the occasion to be, whether there will be entertainment, and what kind it will be. (All of these items will be dealt with later on in this book—don't worry!) Getting a handle on the type of reunion you're going to have, though, is key to working out the rest of the details. Which type you choose depends on a few factors:

- How much time do you have to plan?
- How much money do you have to spend?
- Will others be contributing financially or in other ways?
- How many family members do you estimate will want to attend?
- Will they be coming from far away?

With these things in mind, let's take a look at each of the reunion types in a little more detail.

Clan Clues

Not sure what kind of party to have? Take a look at your holiday card list. How many family members are on it and how far away do they live? This is a great way to give yourself a working idea of how many people you'll need to invite and, more important, what kind of reunion you'll have.

Clown Car or Party Star?

There's nothing nicer for a party than the comforts of your own home—assuming you have enough of those comforts to easily seat, feed, and entertain a pile of people. If you think you want to hold your family reunion in your home, you need to assess your surroundings. The last thing you want is to cram everyone in so tightly that your reunion more closely resembles a clown car in a three-ring circus than a comfortable stroll down the family memory lane.

One great way to keep your stress level down as an at-home host and involve others in the fun of the reunion is to make it potluck. Ask several family members to bring a dish so the burden of feeding the troops isn't all on you. Make sure you designate who's bringing what, though—you don't want to wind up with 25 bowls of potato salad!

Parties held in the home are best suited to smaller, informal gatherings of 10 to 50 for obvious reasons: Unless you live in a mansion on 100 sprawling acres, you simply will not have the space to entertain any more than 50 guests, give or take a cousin. In order to decide whether or not your home is suited to your reunion, take into consideration the following things:

- How many common areas you have available in your home
- How big and how well equipped your kitchen is
- Whether or not you have a backyard or deck space
- How many bathrooms you have and any iffy plumbing issues (an overflowing cesspool smack in the middle of the afternoon won't make for good family photos)
- Whether or not you can accommodate overnight guests who are coming from far away

If you have a backyard, that will add some much-needed elbow room to your at-home shindig. Plus, if there are children involved (and likely there will be), they'll have a lot more fun running off their youthful energy outside with their cousins than sitting indoors stuck to a chair. If you plan on using your outdoor space, check your yard for any potential hazards such as holes in the lawn or neighborhood animals that you see more often roaming unleashed than being walked by their owners. Consider whether you live near a highly trafficked road (potentially dangerous if children will be playing outdoors). You'll also want to check whether your neighborhood has any noise ordinance rules to consider (and you'll definitely want to forewarn your neighbors, especially if you plan on trying out those new outdoor speakers you just got).

Say Uncle!

If you're holding a reunion in your home and young children will be present, make sure you do a safety check of the premises. Put safety plugs in outlets, make sure medicines and poisonous or harmful cleaning agents are safely put away, stow sharp or breakable objects out of reach, set up safety gates to block potentially treacherous staircases, and tack down area rugs to avoid slips and falls.

If your yard will accommodate one, consider renting a tent for your at-home reunion. Although this can be pricey, it's still a less-expensive option than renting a hall or other spot to gather the family, and a tent will prevent sunstroke or rain from throwing a monkey wrench into the day.

Before you agree to host the roast at your home, think over your options carefully and make sure that none of these considerations will be an issue.

You may think to yourself, "Oh, it'll all work out fine!" but you don't want to find yourself—and your guests—spending more time climbing over each other than spending quality time together.

Home *Off* the Range

If your reunion guest list is likely to exceed the 50-person mark, consider an off-site party. Why? Well, besides the obvious reason (space, that is), when the numbers swell, so does the amount of work that goes into the party. It's a lot easier to clean up after 20 people in your home than 100!

You have many options for an off-site reunion. You can hold it at any of the following:

- A local park
- A beach
- A restaurant
- A hotel (a good option if there will be guests coming from far away who'll need a place to stay)
- A catering hall

Of course, holding a reunion off-site with more participants means more work, but as long as you give yourself the recommended time to pull the event together (six months to a year), you should be able to do this with ease. (There's more on organization and planning in Chapter 3, "Get Organized!" as well as ideas on where to have your reunion in Chapter 7, "A Question of Con-gregation.")

Say Uncle!

> If you go to all the trouble of planning
> and arranging a lovely day-in-the-park
> reunion, and forget to contact your local
> parks department for the proper permission
> or permit, you may find yourselves gath-
> ered with nowhere to go. Public parks
> and beaches are, of course, open to any-
> one at almost any time, but larger groups
> generally require special permission. Don't
> forget to get it!

The Weekend-Long Hoedown

When your numbers swell over the 100-person
mark, seriously consider planning your reunion as a
weekend-long event. Why? Quite simply, with all
those guests there just won't be enough hours in a
single afternoon for everyone to spend time together. If folks are going to be coming from all
over, they're going to want to make the most of it.

Of course, this type of reunion takes a lot more
planning (a year to a year and a half). You need to
secure a site that will not only accommodate your
party needs (seating, music, food, outdoor recreational facilities, and so on), but also your guests. If
the site doesn't have sleeping options, at the very
least you should investigate nearby lodging options.

One word of caution: Make sure that you get all arrangements and agreements *in writing* between you and any vendors—whether it's a caterer, the person making up the reunion T-shirts, or the hotel you've decided to use. A handshake isn't good enough, as you'll discover if your reunion day arrives and you find there's a wedding reception being held in the room where *your* party is supposed to be.

What's the Plan, Uncle Stan?

So now you see what I mean about figuring out the plan before you actually start *planning*. A reunion can take on several different forms—a backyard barbecue at your home, a day-long event at a local park or catering hall, or a fun-filled weekend that reunites your far-flung family and gives them time to get reacquainted with each other.

Whichever route you choose to take for your reunion, make sure you have the hours to devote to the plan. If you can't see yourself finding the time to plan a weekend-long reunion, start smaller. You can always build on the work you've done for a smaller reunion to arrange a larger one in the future. You shouldn't feel pressured to do more than you can honestly handle. And besides, the point is to gather the family together, however many you round up. Whether it's 20 or 200 of your kin, your efforts are the best gift of all to your family.

The Least You Need to Know

- The first step in planning a reunion is deciding what kind of party to have.

- If you're thinking about having the party at your home, consider whether you have the space and amenities to easily seat, feed, and entertain 10 to 50 people.

- If you're going to have more than 50 guests, consider holding your celebration at a nearby park, restaurant, or other facility.

- For a guest list that's over 100, a weekend-long reunion makes the trip for faraway relatives worth the while and gives everyone more time to catch up and get re-acquainted.

Chapter 2

The Gist of the List

In This Chapter

- Compiling the guest list: Start small and branch out
- The Reunion Notebook and other organizational tools
- How volunteers can help you search for missing links
- Hold on to that list!

Sure, sitting around gazing at family photo albums all by yourself can be fun, but one person does not a party make. Long-lasting family memories are created when you all get together and laugh and fight and fuss over each other. ("Remember that time Aunt Selma threw the ambrosia in Uncle Artie's lap?! Hoo-hoooo!! That was a hoot!")

But who do you invite? And where do you start? In this chapter, I'll help you to begin your list, find far-flung family members, and get the word out to all your kin. Get your pen ready or your fingers on the keyboard—it's time to start naming names.

Every (Family) Tree Starts as a Seed

Deciding who to invite might not seem like a big deal. After all, by now you have a better idea of what *kind* of reunion you're going to have, so you may already be forming a guest list in your head. But this, too, takes some thought and planning. That's why it's vital to start early and give yourself time to track down all the usual (and unusual) suspects.

Depending on the type of reunion you're prepared to plan—whether it's an informal gathering for 10 or a weekend-long celebration for 200—your list will vary in level of difficulty. However, no matter which type of reunion you plan on, it's best to start with the familiar. Just like Dorothy beginning her journey to Oz at the curvy tip of the Yellow Brick Road, you, too, should begin at the beginning—in this case, your closest relatives who you see on a regular basis. This means your immediate family (mother, father, grandparents, brothers, and sisters). From there, you can list first cousins, second cousins, and so on.

Of course, you may only have a relationship with your immediate family and may not even be sure who your first cousins *are*, due to family rifts, moves, or just your average busy life. It's when you run into these conundrums that the sleuthing begins (I'll discuss this in more detail a little later in this chapter). But in the meantime, let's get you organized.

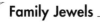

Family Jewels

The Family. We were a strange little band of characters trudging through life sharing diseases and toothpaste, coveting one another's desserts, hiding shampoo, borrowing money, locking each other out of our rooms, inflicting pain and kissing to heal it in the same instant, loving, laughing, defending, and trying to figure out the common thread that bound us all together.

—Erma Bombeck, *The Ties That Bind ... and Gag!* (1987)

The Reunion Tool Kit

To get your list in order (as well as the rest of your reunion plans), you will need a few handy-dandy tools at your disposal:

- A three-ring binder with dividers and storage pockets
- Several different-colored pens or highlighters
- A timetable or calendar (more on how to create a timetable in Chapter 3, "Get Organized!")

What's so great about these tools? They'll keep you on top of (1) who you've invited, (2) when you

invited them, and (3) whether or not they've responded. You'll understand why this is vital when
you're eating leftover lasagna six months after the
reunion has passed because you *thought* you'd have
100 guests, and you ended up having only 10!

You'll use your Reunion Notebook (as I'll call it
from this point on) for many things, but right now
let's concentrate on the sections that relate to your
guest list.

The Book That Binds

Why a binder, you ask? This isn't algebra, for
heaven's sake. The answer is, simply, to get organized. Instead of having a million little pieces of
paper with everyone's phone numbers, addresses,
and e-mails strewn around your house (unless, of
course, you're just one of those folks who naturally
does things like organizing your sock drawer into
color, occasion, season, and date purchased so as to
not wear some out before others), you must beat
your unorganized tendencies into submission.

When taking on a project like planning a family
reunion—no matter how large or small—you'll
have a much easier time keeping track of the clan if
you have one spot where you know you can always
go to reference who, what, when, where, and why.
Trust me, you will come to find your Reunion
Notebook indispensable. You may even experience
separation anxiety when you're away from it. (I
won't tell anyone if you sleep with it under your
pillow at night!) But seriously, one of the best

things you can do for yourself as the planner of this shindig is to keep your plans in one spot, starting with the guest list. You—and your relatives, some of whom may be traveling miles to see you—will be happy you did.

Crayons Aren't Just for Kids

Don't laugh—a color-coding system can make the difference between keeping tabs on the pack and losing track of who's calling whom, who's coming, and who will be a no-show. Especially when planning a larger reunion, a color-coding system can be a real time saver. There are a couple of ways to use this system, depending on what works best for you. You can use magic markers or you can make your list in regular old ballpoint pen and then just use different colored highlighters to symbolize you and your helpers.

In the instance of larger reunions, you are going to want to get some help tracking down and inviting family members (more on soliciting volunteers later in this chapter) and it's very easy to forget who's doing what.

Let's say you've asked your Aunt Iris and your cousin Susan to help you with the guest list, which consists of around 150 relatives. You've divided up the list among the three of you. By assigning each of you a color, you'll have an easy, quick-reference way to keep track of who's in charge of inviting whom and what the results are.

Let's say you're red, cousin Susan is green, and Aunt Iris is blue. The names on the list that each of you is in charge of will be written in these designated colors, creating an automatic signal to you every time you open the book. If there's no note next to long-lost Uncle Jeb's name and you can't remember why, you'll know that if the name is in green, you can just call up your cousin Susan to find out what the story is. Don't forget to provide each of your volunteers with a color-coded list, too. That way, everyone will stay up to speed on who's doing what.

Say Uncle!

Why not just divide the names into separate lists and hand those out? Not a good idea. Instead of having to keep track of one all-encompassing list of names, you'll have to keep track of two or more (depending on how many volunteers you solicit). Plus, if each of your volunteers has only the names that concern them, they won't be able to help track someone down whose name appears on another list.

Keeping Track of Time

A clear time plan and a calendar will be absolutely indispensable in your reunion planning. And, lucky you, with the help of a little gadget called a three-hole punch, you can easily slap them into your Reunion Notebook. No matter what kind of reunion you are planning, having a clearly drawn-out time scheme is very important.

Besides the reunion date, there are other dates that will be important. As far as your list goes, these dates will have to do with when you send out your first, second, and possibly third set of announcements (yes, you'll need to send out more than just the official invite!), as well as what your cut-off dates are for responses (so you'll know when to start asking people whether they plan on attending).

Any Volunteers?

As I've mentioned, fleshing out your large guest list is a lot easier if you solicit a few volunteers. Why? Well, all your kin may well not be on your holiday card list and therefore their information not readily at your fingertips. If your family has moved around a lot or had some silly spats, it's entirely possible you've lost track of some of your relatives.

For example, years after Wendy's mom passed away, Wendy decided that she wanted to have a reunion for her mom's side of the family. After her mom's death, she lost touch with her mother's only cousin, as well as his two children—key links in her family's chain. Wendy solicited the help of her uncle, who readily had the information she was looking for, as well as contact information for several other family members Wendy hadn't seen since she was a child. Once she contacted them, it snowballed. She found more and more first cousins, which led to second cousins and third cousins, all because she used her family's network to her sleuthing advantage.

 Clan Clues _____

> Not only does soliciting volunteers lighten your workload, it's also a fun, bonding activity that you can do together as family members that will make the reunion that much more memorable.

You may be shy about asking for help, but get over it—and fast. The fact is, your family will likely embrace the project. It's not only help for you, but an activity that will be added to your reunion memories (as well as your database of family names for the next time you hold a reunion).

Keeping Tabs on Your Volunteers

Of course, as the organizer, you're going to need to oversee your troops. You should try to do the following:

- Divide your family "branches" into categories (uncles and aunts, cousins, greats, and so on). For instance, if your father's cousin Marv has more access to information about the array of cousins on that side, solicit his expertise in tracking them down. If your Aunt Mary knows more about the great aunts and uncles, let her concentrate on that.

- Set aside a day each week where your volunteers call or send in progress reports and update your main list accordingly. E-mail can be particularly helpful here. In fact, you'll find e-mail and the Internet are invaluable tools for your reunion from start to finish. If all of your volunteers have e-mail accounts, you can send out e-mail to everyone without having to retype their addresses each time. Also, the Internet offers many tools you can use to search for your long-losts, which I'll cover in Chapter 4, "Untangling the Web."

- Once you've updated the list, make sure you give copies of it to your volunteers. That way, no one will double up on work already done (after all, there's no time to waste!), and if one family member is running into a snag tracking someone down, another member might be able to help out.

- Make sure contact information for each of your volunteers (full name, phone, e-mail, address, and immediate family members) appear on the updated lists. That way, no one will have to waste time looking for contact info—it will always be readily available.

- Use the color-coding system that I discussed earlier in this chapter!

Sniffing Out Other Clues

You've heard the old family ribbing that the only time everyone really gets together is at weddings and funerals. Although this tends to be true in many a clan, there is one thing that is commonly found at both of these events: a sign-in book.

Clan Clues

Have you ever made fun of your mom's pack-rat habits? You know, she saves every little card and the envelope it came in from your relatives from birth to birthdays to graduations and every little event in between? Use them! Old envelopes and correspondence are great tools for tracking down relatives you haven't heard from in years.

Between you and your volunteers, dig out any sign-in books from family gatherings that you may have in your possession. See if you can get your hands on those from other family members as well. Frequently, these books not only contain names but addresses of family members who have been in attendance. Even if an address is not included, you will be able to find the names of distant cousins and others with whom you may have fallen out of touch or don't really know at all. The sign-in book is a good (and often overlooked) starting point for fleshing out the reunion guest list. Those who tend to show up for these occasions will more than likely want to be contacted about a family get-together (especially one that's taking place under purely happy circumstances).

Other good, under-your-nose sources of names, faces, and addresses include the following:

- **Holiday card lists.** If your card list isn't up to snuff or if you don't send cards, ask another family member for this list.

- **Recent birth announcements.** If you or any of your volunteers recently brought a new member into the family—or know of a family member who did—use the birth-announcement mailing list as part of your resource material.

- **Family photo albums.** Searching for faces in family photo albums is another good sleuthing source. People will often record details about the photo on the back. But if not, process of elimination can work, too. For instance, maybe you recognize Aunt Edna in that old black-and-white shot from the 1940s, but who's that guy standing next to her? Call Aunt Edna and ask!

If you and your volunteers have compiled the basic list but still need to fill in some holes, try sending out a questionnaire to all those family members for whom you have contact information. It can be a simple one-page affair that asks for the known names and addresses of additional family members who might not be on the list. Be sure to include a self-addressed, stamped envelope to ensure that they send it back!

 Family Jewels

> We all grow up with the weight of history on us. Our ancestors dwell in the attics of our brains as they do in the spiraling chains of knowledge hidden in every cell of our bodies.
>
> —Shirley Abbot, *Womenfolks: Growing Up Down South* (1983)

All Buildings Start with a Foundation

You've tracked down aunts, uncles, cousins, and greats from far and wide and created an extensive list of family members. Once the reunion is over, don't just sigh to yourself, "Boy, was that a lot fun!" and toss out the list! That was a lot of hard work you did, and this list of family members can be useful in the future.

First and foremost, if you or any of your other family members decide to do this again (or even make the reunion an annual event), that list will be priceless. Even if you only had a small reunion, the names and information you gathered for it will be the building blocks for the next time around. (In Chapter 4, I'll tell you about some interactive Internet tools you can use to keep your family's information constantly updated.)

Of course, this is worth more than just keeping your list updated. It will allow family members to get and remain in touch with each other and ensure that your family's past, present, and future remain a living entity.

The Least You Need to Know

- When starting your guest list, start small and, depending on the size of reunion you're having, climb farther out onto the family branches.

- Creating a Reunion Notebook will keep your guest list (and your planning in general) neat, organized, and easily accessible.

- Solicit help from other family members. Not only will it save you time and headaches, it's a great way to extend the fun of the reunion and create new memories.

- Don't throw out your list! All that hard work and research will come in handy again someday, whether it's to plan another reunion or just to keep in touch with your kin.

Chapter 3

Get Organized!

In This Chapter

- Setting the reunion date—and sticking to it
- Create a timetable for a small reunion
- Create a timetable for a larger reunion
- Create a timetable for a weekend reunion

The names have been named—you and your volunteers have researched yourselves into a reunion roster you're all happy with. Now what? The "when," of course!

But with the "when" comes a bunch of other little "when's" during the course of your planning that, once designated, will help you keep your planning on target and organized all the way up to the main event. In this chapter I'll help you plot out the best day for your reunion and create a timeline to keep track of all the little details.

Deciding on the Date

The biggest rule for date-setting is this: Once you choose a date, stick with it. Whatever you do, don't flim-flam around changing dates to try and accommodate everyone. Know right here and now that you will *never* be able to make the whole clan happy. There will likely be some folks who simply can't make it due to other obligations. If you try to bend over backwards to make everyone happy, you'll not only cause yourself a lot of stress, you may create quite a bit of confusion. The last thing you want are relatives showing up the week before the actual reunion because they got an old date mixed up with the final one.

Family Jewels _____

> Call it a clan, call it a network, call it a tribe, call it a family. Whatever you call it, whoever you are, you need one.

This is not to say that you should declare, "To heck with everyone!" and pick whatever day sounds good to you. In fact, you can use one of your handy-dandy list research tools from Chapter 2, "The Gist of the List," to help you out here. Remember the family questionnaire I suggested you send out? In it, you can also include several possible reunion dates from which to pick. When you get the questionnaires back you can tally up the answers and settle on the one date that best suits the general consensus.

In addition, there are two more things to consider when deciding on the calendar mark for your reunion:

1. Do you want the reunion to coincide with a special date such as an anniversary, holiday, or birthday?

2. Is there a particular time of year that's better or more convenient to hold your reunion?

Your Secret Weapon: The Timetable

Are you starting to feel the slightest flush of panic rising in your cheeks? Are you thinking, "Oh heavens, what have I gotten myself into?!" Now, now. It's not that hard. Well, okay, there *is* a lot that goes into pulling off a successful reunion and you, as organizer, are the one everyone will turn to with questions, conundrums, and other such quandaries. But there's a secret weapon to keeping your cool, reunion wrangler. It's called a timetable. Once you've accomplished a task, you can just check the box next to that task. Go down the list of tasks, and before you know it, you're done—let the party begin!

Your timetable will vary depending on what kind of event you are planning to undertake—a small gathering at home, a larger gathering at a rented spot, or a weekend-long extravaganza. But guess what? I'm going to walk you through each and every one. Ready? Get a calendar and let's set the dates.

Small Reunion Timetable

For a small reunion, you should be able to easily gel your plan within three to six months. The following plan allows for the maximum amount of time, which I highly recommend you use. However, you can easily tailor this plan to three months, because a small reunion requires less time spent rounding up your kin.

Six months before the reunion:

❏ Do an informal poll of those family members whom you are in touch with to feel them out—are they interested in having a reunion?

❏ Create your Reunion Notebook (see Chapter 2), where you'll record all important information regarding the reunion.

❏ Make your family guest list (for a small reunion, this is much easier to do right off the bat).

❏ Solicit one or two volunteers, if you need them.

❏ Assess your home—can you hold the reunion there? If not, find a willing family member's home or other venue that's more suitable.

❑ Decide on the basic menu. Be sure to include your volunteers in this decision—food is always fun! (See Chapter 9, in "Dig In!" for more on menu planning.)

❑ Select two or three potential reunion dates.

Five months before the reunion:

❑ Call or e-mail family members to take a poll of the date options.

❑ Double-check that mailing information is up to date.

❑ Based on your basic menu, ask if any family members would be willing to contribute a dish. (If it's an old family recipe, all the better—see Chapter 10, "Eat, Drink, and Be Family," for more on how to incorporate family recipes into your reunion.)

❑ Settle on a date. (Remember, stick to it!)

❑ Assess how many guests will be bringing dishes.

❑ If you are going to need to rent chairs, tables, a tent, or cater food, start researching your local options and getting prices.

Four months before the reunion:

❑ Create a family newsletter and send it out. This will be your first "mailer" (for a small reunion, you only need two—the newsletter reminding guests of the date and getting them psyched for the family fun, and the actual invitation).

In the newsletter, include phone numbers and addresses for local hotels and car rental companies so out-of-town guests can make their own arrangements (unless your guest list is quite small and you can handle making these arrangements yourself). You might also want to include a map with written directions to the party. If you'll be creating a family cookbook, ask for family recipes, too.

❑ Lock in your chair/table/tent rentals and food catering. Make sure to get all arrangements in writing.

❑ If part or all of your reunion will be held outside, check with your local officials to see if there are any noise ordinances you need to be aware of.

 Clan Clues _____

> If guests will be making family recipes to bring, ask them to bring a copy of the recipe so you can incorporate it into a "Family Recipes Cookbook" that you can distribute to family members after the reunion is over.

Three months before the reunion:

❑ Send out the official invitation.

❑ If the reunion will be held in your home, take care of any needed home improvement projects or repairs (filling in holes in the yard, painting, cleaning carpets, and so on).

Say Uncle!

Make sure your camera or camcorder is working before the day of the event and that it has working batteries. Be sure you have plenty of film on hand, too—you don't want to have to rush off during the festivities to buy more!

Two months before the reunion:

❏ Purchase decorations, disposable utensils, paper plates, cups, a sign-in book, and other supplies (and store them in a place where you won't forget them!).

One month before the reunion:

❏ Assess your supplies—do you have everything you need? Make any last-minute purchases that you may have overlooked the month before.

Two weeks before the reunion:

❏ Call to confirm any rentals or catering arrangements you've made.

One week before the reunion:

❏ Forewarn your neighbors (it's the polite thing to do!).

❏ Shop for groceries.

The day before the reunion:

❏ Clean the house, move any furniture that needs to be moved, put up decorations.

❏ If you can prepare any food ahead of time, do so today.

Reunion day:

❏ Congratulations, you made it! Take some time to relax before the festivities begin—it's going to be a big day!

Larger Reunion Timetable

More people means more planning—figure on six months to a year. Think a year is a lot of time? It's not. You'll need all the time you can get to plan properly. Make your timetable and stick to it—you don't want to end up doing things last minute or, worse, find out some of your plans have been foiled because you didn't allot enough time.

One year before the reunion:

❏ Create your Reunion Notebook.

❏ Start your family guest list.

❏ Solicit two or three family volunteers.

❏ Select three potential reunion dates.

❏ Create and send out a family questionnaire that asks your kin (1) for further family information they may have and (2) to pick from the potential dates for the reunion. (Don't forget to include a self-addressed, stamped envelope and a deadline by which to respond!)

Say Uncle! _____

Don't be afraid to ask for donations! More than likely, your family members will be happy to contribute to the fund or to the supplies you'll need. Be sure to note a deadline in your newsletter to turn in cash donations so you'll have money on hand to pay for deposits, rentals, and so on. It's also a good idea to set up a "reunion account" at the bank to keep track of your spending.

Ten months before the reunion:

❏ From the questionnaires you've received back, decide on a date.

❏ Lock in your reunion site. If you'll be holding the reunion in a public place such as a park, make sure you apply for any necessary permits and find out whether or not alcohol is permitted if you plan on serving it.

❑ Using the family information from the questionnaires, solidify your guest list and divide up the names among your volunteers so they can fill in any missing information.

❑ Create a family newsletter and send out to guests informing them of the date and any other pertinent information (such as lodging and car rental options, family recipe solicitations, and donation solicitations).

 Clan Clues _____

> Many hotels will give lower-rate package deals for large groups. Investigate the best deals and include the names of those hotels in your newsletter. When guests call the hotel to book a reservation, they can ask for the "so-and-so party" to get the special rate.

Nine months before the reunion:

❑ Plan your activities for the reunion. If there will be entertainment, get it locked in (and get the arrangements in writing).

❑ If you plan to hire a photographer, research your options and book him or her.

❑ Research catering options and book them.

❑ If there is a family member(s) who you would like to give a speech at the reunion, contact this person so he or she has enough time to put together the speech.

Six to eight months before the reunion:

❏ Design/order family T-shirts or other favors.

❏ If you'll be creating a family cookbook, put together the recipes and drop them off at a local printer. (You might want to ask a volunteer to handle this whole process, freeing you up to concentrate on other things.)

❏ If you'll need to rent a tent, tables, chairs, etc., make sure you lock this in now.

❏ Send out a save-the-date reminder postcard to guests. (For an in-between mailer, postcards are a much less expensive option than letters, because they are cheaper to buy and the postage is less, too!)

Four months before the reunion:

❏ Purchase decorations; any disposable utensils, paper plates, and cups you'll need if they aren't being supplied by the caterer; a sign-in book; extra film and batteries; and whatever else you might need (and store them in a place where you won't forget them!).

❏ Send out an official reunion invitation (don't forget to give guests an RSVP date!).

Two months before the reunion:

❏ Follow up with any stragglers on the guest list who haven't yet committed to the date.

❏ Assess your supplies—do you have everything you need? Make any last-minute purchases that you may have overlooked.

One month before the reunion:

❏ Call to confirm any rental arrangements you've made.

❏ If you're going to need coolers, barbecue grills, or other food-related items, make sure you have any loaners locked in or have purchased what you need.

One week before the reunion:

❏ Put together your favors, welcome packet, nametags, or any giveaway items you want your family to take with them.

❏ If guests will be bringing food or other items, call them to confirm.

❏ Do a dummy check—go through your Reunion Notebook and make sure all outstanding items/questions have been checked off.

The day before the reunion:

❏ Tomorrow's the big day, so schedule some time to relax!

Reunion day:

❏ You and your volunteers should arrive early to make sure everything at the site is A-OK (rentals have arrived, decorations are in place, food is set up, reunion takeaways are placed where family members can readily see and take them, and so on), as well as to greet any early arrivals.

❏ Congratulate yourself on a job well done, and have fun!

Weekend Reunion Timetable

More people plus more party days equals—you guessed it—a few more months on the calendar. The following timetable is the same as the previous Larger Reunion timetable, except that you'll be starting the planning up to six months earlier.

Eighteen months to one year before the reunion:

❏ Create your Reunion Notebook.

❏ Start your family guest list.

❏ Solicit two or three family volunteers.

❏ Select three potential reunion dates.

❏ Create and send out a family questionnaire that asks your kin (1) for further family information they may have and (2) to pick from the potential dates for the reunion. (Don't forget the self-addressed, stamped envelope and a deadline by which to respond!)

From this point on, refer to the previous timetable, starting with 10 months before the reunion.

The Least You Need to Know

- Once you set your date, stick to it. You won't be able to accommodate everyone's schedule, but the sooner you lock in the date, the easier it will be for you and your family members to make plans.

- In deciding on the date, think about the best time of year for your reunion. Would a holiday event or a seasonally planned reunion work best for your clan?

- Create a timetable according to the kind of reunion you plan to have.

- You may think you have lots of time, but get the ball rolling as early as you can. There's nothing more stressful than leaving big decisions to the last minute.

Untangling the Web

In This Chapter

- Why you should use the Internet to help plan your reunion
- Search tools that get the job done
- "Evite" the troops!
- Shop 'til your (fingers) drop
- Create a web page for virtual family congregation

At this point in the twenty-first century, there's no need to sell you on the virtues of the Internet. It seems most everyone is hooked up and surfin' now, and not just the young folks. Many of the older generation are finding that the Internet and e-mail are a great way to keep in touch with family and friends on a regular basis. You could even make a strong case for the Internet bringing families closer together. Suddenly, California to New York is but a click away instead of a 3,000-mile plane ride.

Even better, you can use this invaluable tool to seek out, hook up, and bring together your clan, as well as find some pretty cool stuff to make your reunion planning a little bit easier. In this chapter, we're going on a surfin' safari—get ready to catch the wave!

Destination Dot Com

Whether you're searching for that long-lost uncle or trying to scout out the perfect spot to have your reunion, the Internet is a fantastic source of information literally at your fingertips. Let's get up close and e-personal with some great site info to help you plan for your clan.

Seek and Greet

Whether you're trying to keep tabs on those usual family members or are trying to find some long-lost kin, using the Internet can cut down on time and hassle. However, keep this one caveat in mind: You are not going to magically find everyone in your family this way. Yes, there are many useful (and free!) tools available on the web, but you are more than likely going to have to also use the phone, ye olde Post Office, and your network of family volunteers to help you in your search for family members (see Chapter 2, "The Gist of the List").

Say Uncle!

Many people-searching websites will draw you in with claims of being a free service, when in fact to get any actual information you'll need to pay a fee (and it's not guaranteed anything will turn up). There are several good free sites and organizations out there that won't ask you for a red cent, so before spending money on a search service, make sure you really need to fork over that cash.

Following are some great free sites that can help you track down those who have eluded your holiday card list up until now:

- **Yahoo! People Search (people.yahoo. com).** This database gives you access to everyone listed in every phonebook nationwide, and also does e-mail address searches. Unfortunately, if someone isn't listed somewhere, somehow, they won't turn up here. But it's a good starting point for finding those with whom you've lost touch.

- **Google (www.google.com).** Google is a great site for tracking down what someone's been up to and, hopefully, can give you clues as to how to find them. When you "google" someone's name, all web records of that person are displayed for you to browse through. Google also features a people search that shows publicly listed phone numbers and addresses.

- **FindAgain.com (www.findagain.com).** On this site, you supply information (your name and e-mail address) and then enter the details of the person you're searching for. When and if your long-lost visits the site, a message will pop up for them saying that you are looking for them. However, unless the person you're looking for has signed up with the site, you won't find him or her here.

One drawback to using these sites is that if the name you're searching for is a common one, you may have to sift through a lot of information about other people before you can parse out the person for whom you are searching. Knowing the middle name or initial, the city in which the person lives, or other personal details can help narrow down your search results.

That said, using these sites is an excellent addition to the rest of your sleuthing techniques and can cut down on your search time. (In Chapter 12, "Shaking the Family Tree," I'll take this one step further and help you use the Internet and other tools to trace your genealogy and dig up information on your family's past!)

You're Evited!

Using the Internet to electronically invite your family to your reunion is an easy, fun way to supplement (and save a little money on) your guest list. Check out the free services offered by these websites:

- **Evite.com (www.evite.com).** The big momma of all evite services, this site allows you to create an address book of your recipients; take an electronic poll of your guests' preferences for time, date, and place; send out reminders; and post photos. It also links your guests to Citysearch.com if they're coming from far away and need lodging, offers a map and directions, and has a feature called PayPal that allows your guests to make financial contributions to the party (nice!).

- **Regards.com (www.regards.com).** This site lets you send evites up to 14 months before an event. Even better, you can log on today and predate the invitation, selecting a future date on which you wish to have the invitation sent. There's not a huge selection of invitations and none are family-specific; however, you can personalize them with your own message. You can also track your guests' RSVPs.

- **eSprings.com (www.esprings.com).** This site allows you to create an occasion, track

RSVPs, make an address book, resend invitations to those who haven't responded, provide a map and directions to the occasion, send thank you notes, and put up postparty pictures of your event.

- **Sendomatic.com (www.sendomatic.com).** This site has its own family reunion category and allows you to create an address books of invitees, track RSVPs, provide maps and directions, and tell guests what to bring to the shindig.

- **Yahoo! Invites (invites.yahoo.com).** This site has a special reunion category of invitations. It allows you to create an address book; track RSVPs; poll guests on date, site, and time; create an event web page; and put up postparty photos. It also provides maps and directions, and a message board on which your guests can post comments and questions.

Have Credit Card, Will Shop

Making purchases online can be a little scary. Although it's becoming more and more common to shop online, the fact that you never look someone in the eye as you're forking over your plastic is a leap of faith for many of us.

Never fear, you can shop online with confidence! When making purchases online, just be sure a little "lock" symbol appears at the bottom of the page. This means that you are buying merchandise over a secure server; that is, no one but you and the company can view your purchase information and your credit card information, is safe.

Clan Clues

Found a great website to get those all-important reunion T-shirts, but still feel a little funny about giving out your credit card number? Check out the Better Business Bureau's great new online shopping site at www.bbbonline.org/consumer to see if the company you want to buy from is on the up-and-up.

However, there is something very quick and painless about going online, browsing through some merchandise, and purchasing it from the comfort of your own home with a few clicks of the mouse. Let's take a look at some of the items you may well want to consider purchasing online for your reunion:

- **Favors.** Whether it's T-shirts or golf tees, it's fun and easy to find all kinds of family-reunion favors online. Many of the companies you'll find actually use their website to supplement their actual "store-front" business.

- **Party supplies.** From preprinted banners to helium balloons to invitations, there are many reputable party-supply sites for one-stop online shopping.

- **Hotels.** Most major hotels have a website that allows you to make queries regarding room availability and cost as well as reservations.

- **Plane tickets.** You can use online plane ticket services (or check the websites of the major airlines) to find out prices, check availability, reserve flights, and put flights on hold (usually for up to 24 hours).

Listing the sites here will take up more space then we've got in this chapter, but turn to Appendix A, "Web and Software Resources," for some great places to start.

 Family Jewels

Technology evolves so much faster than wisdom.

—Jennifer Stone, *Mind over Media* (1988)

Virtual Congregation

One of the best things the Internet has done for the world at large is to bring people a little closer together. When you find your East-Coast self chatting weekly via e-mail with your West-Coast uncle (who, previously, you talked with once a year if you were lucky), you can't deny the value of this technology. It may not make your family less strange, but it certainly makes you feel less like strangers.

For your reunion—and maybe even more important, long after it's over—there are several family websites offering free services that will allow you to keep everyone up to date on reunion news, as well as personal family bits to keep you all in the loop on each other's lives:

- **MyFamily.com (www.myfamily.com).** This site allows you to create your family's very own page. It's free and fairly simple to do and, although not in "real" chat time, lets you and your family keep in touch. After the reunion, you can post pictures of your family get-together so you can all see what a good time everyone had. It's a great tool to use for planning the next one, too! This site also allows members to post their respective birthdays and sends a reminder out to the rest of the clan not to forget those dates.

- **OurFamily.com (www.ourfamily.com).** Here, you can create you family's own website where you can make use of a calendar (to help plan your reunion, of course), photo archives, and real-time chat.

- **Better Homes and Gardens (www.bhg. com).** From the tried-and-true home gurus comes a family website-building tool to help you keep in touch with the clan. From their main website just type in "Family Reunions" to pull up several links to helpful articles.

- **America Online Groups (www. groups@aol.com).** Here you can create a "group" (for example, Smith Reunion) where you and your family can post messages to each other as well as family photos.

The Least You Need to Know

- Using online search tools can help you save time (and money!) when it comes to seeking out long-lost family members.

- Evite services are a handy way to get the reunion word out as well as send reminders and allow the troops to post questions about the upcoming party.

- While you may be a little dubious about making purchases online, with the advent of secure servers it is safe to give out your credit card information.

- There are several free, easy online tools to help you create a family website, and it's a great way to keep the whole family involved in the reunion fun.

Chapter 5

News You Can Use

In This Chapter

- Start the family presses!
- What should go in a family newsletter
- Other mailables to keep family members in the loop
- Creating a family address book

Get it in print, that's what your Uncle Olaf always used to say. Not bad advice, certainly when it comes to reunions. The printed word is an entertaining, productive way to get out the details of your family fandango as well as get everyone in the reunion spirit.

Here you'll learn how to put together a fun, fact-packed newsletter and create an all-encompassing family address book, as well as create other handy handouts and mailers that everyone will be happy to see in their mailbox.

What's in a Newsletter

When you hear the word "newsletter," do you automatically find yourself yawning as visions of boring, irrelevant stacks of information dance in your head? Do you picture those sleep-inducing corporate updates or those impersonal holiday letters from people telling you about the new tricks their dog learned this year or that they bought new tires for the SUV?

Well, then, you've just never read a good one.

A prereunion family newsletter can do a lot of things. It can:

- Act as a "save the date" notice.
- Give important travel information to help your faraway family members plan ahead.
- Entertain with fun family facts.
- Give information about contests and games guests may want to prepare for before the reunion.
- Update everyone on intriguing family news.
- Ask for reunion-related contributions (photos, recipes, stories, and the all-important cash!).

Let's take a closer look at what you can put in your newsletter to make it fun and interesting for your recipients to read.

News Your Family Can Use

If you plan to send a newsletter to inform guests of an upcoming reunion (and I highly recommend you do!), there are a few pieces of information that it must contain: the date of the party, where it will be held, and how to get there. In fact, those first two points should be the first pieces of information recipients see when they open your little slice of journalistic perfection.

Your newsletter should begin with a large, eye-catching heading that nobody can miss. Here's an example:

FIRST ANNUAL FISHER FAMILY FUN FEST!

SATURDAY, JUNE 20, 2003

4 P.M. 'til 10 P.M.

The Springhouse Restaurant

Rochester, New York

Other vital bits that you'll want to have early on in the newsletter is travel information, such as the following:

- Directions! If you can include a map of the area in the newsletter, all the better. If not, detailed driving directions from the major thoroughfares will do fine.
- A list of hotels and other lodging options in the area, their contact information, and whether or not a hotel is offering rooms at a discounted group rate.

- Bus, train, taxi, car rental, and air information. This should include contact information (telephone numbers and web addresses) for the major public transportation venues in the area.

Of course, if you're planning an informal reunion with only a small group of family members, and you know they'll all be driving to the reunion or they all live close by, you can skip some of this information. But otherwise, why is it important to include this stuff? If you can look it all up, why can't they? As the planner of this party, and as someone who knows the area, you want to ensure that as many family members as possible show up and enjoy the festivities. Anything you can do to simplify matters now will save you, and everyone else, time and aggravation later on. The day of the reunion you don't want to be fielding 50 phone calls from geographically challenged relatives who never bothered to look at a map, or who arrive expecting to stay overnight in your home.

 **Clan Clues**

If you belong to AAA, take advantage of their free mapping service for road travel that gives quick, spot-on directions. If you have Internet access, check out Mapquest (www.mapquest.com), which is another excellent source for maps and directions for getting from point A to point B.

What's Happenin'?

Your newsletter should also include information on family events that will be held during the festivities. Not only does this give everyone a preview of the fun to come, it allows them to prepare or rummage around for items that may be required during the reunion.

You should try to include a basic itinerary of the day or weekend, as well as details on specific events that may require more preparation. For instance, if you plan on having a cook-off or just want folks to contribute family recipes to the cookbook you're putting together, you'll want to include these details so your guests can plan accordingly.

If you're asking family members to contribute photos for a family album, they'll need a little time to dig through their albums and shoeboxes, and possibly make copies of the pictures if they don't want to let go of the originals. You might also be thinking about putting together a book of family lore (see Chapter 13, "Once Upon a Clan," for more on this topic). If so, family members may want to polish their stories to make sure they're just so.

The More (Info), the Merrier

Once you get the important details out of the way, you may want to include interesting, fun family information to get everyone into the reunion spirit. For instance, if you've done some genealogy research (see Chapter 12, "Shaking the Family Tree"), you've no doubt learned some interesting facts about your clan. Why not include some of them? You can put this information in a separate "Did You Know …?" section, or scatter these notes throughout the newsletter in the form of sidebars. Experiment with some eye-catching designs!

In addition, you can use the newsletter to keep your family informed of any happenings within your clan. Sharing news of graduations, births, anniversaries, and other happy milestones keeps everyone in on the family grapevine.

 Say Uncle!

Packing your newsletter full of important and entertaining information is great, but don't let it run too long. Aim for a maximum of two double-sided pages. If there's too much information, some important information might get lost in the shuffle.

Cash and Kin

The final thing you'll want to include in closing your newsletter is a request for financial contributions if you plan on asking for them. Here, you should …

- Make your request.
- Tell your family members exactly what the money will be used for (deposit on the site, food, entertainment, etc.).

- Include contact information for where to send donations, or the bank and "family account number" for direct deposits (if a branch of the bank is available in most areas).

- Give a deadline. Of course, this does not mean contributions can't be made after the fact, but a deadline will make sure that the funds are available for all the deposits and petty cash needed ahead of time.

If you feel a little uncomfortable asking for money, remember: This event is for the *whole* family. Everyone will enjoy the event and, chances are, most will happy to contribute.

More for the Mailbag

In addition to your family newsletter, you may want to think about sending out a few other pieces of mail, depending on the size and type of reunion you're planning:

- **Reminder postcards.** Postcards are short, sweet, and cheap! They're a great way to remind your family members about the reunion date as it nears (and hey, it's always nice to get fun mail instead of a bill!).

- **An information packet.** If you have the resources and the time, consider taking your newsletter a step farther and sending out a full-on information packet filled with road maps, public transportation maps, area recreational information, hotel brochures, and any other local information you think might be useful.

● **Blank recipe cards.** Include these to encourage those who've signed up for any cooking-related activities to write down their recipe on the card and bring it with them. If you want, the cards can be personalized for your family ("A Fisher Family Recipe"). If you send out an information packet, you can easily include these in it.

● **Family tree sheets.** If you're researching your genealogy but have come up against some missing branches on the family tree, it's helpful (and fun!) to get the rest of the family involved in the search. Sending these sheets out before the reunion gives your family members some time to look into your collective roots. Then they can complete the family tree sheets and bring them to the reunion. There's more about this in Chapter 12.

Family Jewels

Our correspondences have wings—paper birds that fly from my house to yours.

—Terry Tempest Williams, *Refuge* (1991)

Where Are They Now?

You've spent a lot of time and effort tracking down your family members and recording that information. Wouldn't it be a shame if all your hard work went to waste? It doesn't have to. Why not create a family address book to give out to your clan on reunion day? You've already done the hard work; all you really might have to do is photocopy your guest information list from your Reunion Notebook, assemble the information in binders or staple it together, and voilà! A family address book. Of course, you can get a little fancier, if you like. One way to make the family address book even more of a keepsake is to order extra copies of the reunion photos and include a picture next to the family member's name. That way, if your family is particularly large there will be a name/face association. Also, seeing photos from the day brings back good memories and hits that soft spot we all have in our hearts.

The Least You Need to Know

- A family newsletter is a practical and fun way to keep the whole group involved in the reunion plans.
- Don't forget to include the vitals in a prominent place in the newsletter: when, where, and how to get there!
- Consider sending out additional information, such as family tree sheets or recipe cards, for even more fun.
- Create a family address book and keep the reunion spirit going all year long.

Problem Children

In This Chapter

- To invite or not to invite?
- Getting shy guests involved in the fun
- How to make reluctant spouses feel comfortable
- Heading off problems

Last week you got a phone call from Aunt Josephine. She was sweet as pie, chattering on and on about this and that and making all kinds of family small talk. But somehow, you got the feeling there was something else on her mind. And then, finally, it came out: "Um, are you inviting your Cousin Joe to the reunion?" Now, this sounded like an innocent enough question, but you knew exactly what she was really saying: "Are you going to invite that troublemaker so he can ruin our family reunion?"

Everybody's got at least one in the family: the black sheep, who always seems to bring a little mischief into the mix. But of course, it's not just the bah-bah black sheep that spell trouble. There's the family grudges, the unresolved squabbles, the so-called "outcasts" whose lifestyles always seem to raise an eyebrow or two, the reluctant spouses who don't exactly relish the idea of spending hours (let alone a few days) with your kin.

So what do you do about this muddy mix of mal-contents at your reunion? Must you spend sleep-less, fret-filled nights worrying about all your hard work and planning being ruined? While you can't expect to mend all family fences, you can use a few peacemaking tactics to help everyone feel welcome and preserve your family's fun and future memories. In this chapter, I'll help you find ways to head off some of the trouble and ensure that a good time is had by all.

 Family Jewels

Family life! The United Nations is child's play compared to the tugs and splits and need to understand and forgive in any family.

—May Sarton, *Kinds of Love* (1970)

Dealing with the Outcasts and Castaways

Just because you're blood relatives doesn't auto-matically mean you're all going to get along famously; in fact, your associations may lean more toward the *in*famous. Add a little controversy to the mix, and your family pot can boil over. Whether it's something as innocuous as the tattoo-and-nipple-piercing antics of Cousin Anthony or the more serious drinking problem of Uncle Al, some family members end up being singled out (or singling themselves out) from the bunch and, thus, stirring up familial controversy.

When it comes to these black sheep in the flock, you may well be asking yourself: Should I invite them at all? Maybe the trouble you envision this invitee causing isn't worth the agony. Well, not so fast. Before you make that decision, think about what it means. Not only are you casting out the supposed offending party, but you are sending him or her a very clear message: You are not welcome in this family.

Do you *really* want to do that?

Clan Clues

Think your family's weird and combative? If smoothing over family ruffles is making you feel a little stressed, rent *Home for the Holidays* for a well-deserved laugh. This hilarious movie, starring Holly Hunter, Anne Bancroft, and Robert Downey Jr. will have you thankful that (hopefully!) your family isn't that bad after all.

You may think the lack of this person's presence will make the party go a lot smoother, but what you need to think about first and foremost is the future. This isn't just about a day or two going off without a hitch—it's about your relationship with this person. Unless you are prepared to sever this tie and you have very, very good reasons to do so, think twice about not including this person. Unless your Cousin Ralph is a known mass murderer, don't exclude him for the sake of convenience. The hurt feelings will be a lot harder (if not impossible) to smooth over than a few moments of discomfort on reunion day.

Besides, reunions are about getting together, not keeping people apart. The decision to come or not should be left in the hands of the person invited. So take a deep breath, put on a big smile, and send out that invitation. You are not responsible for solving all squabbles or preventing future ones. But you *can* welcome everyone with open arms, which may be responsible for a little mending in and of itself.

Shy Cousin Di

Some family members may greet the notion of a family reunion with a less-than-enthusiastic response. You can probably already think of a few of your kin who, for one reason or another, tend toward this type of wallflower status. Whether it's due to an illness, a recent divorce, or maybe they're just plain shy, a little gentle coaxing might be in order. The key word here is, of course, *gentle*.

 Family Jewels

> Fortunately, the family is a human institution: humans made it, and humans can change it.
> —Shere Hite, *The Hite Report on the Family* (1994)

You don't want to overwhelm your shrinking violets. Maybe you're the gregarious type who has no problem making conversation and are the first to jump into any social situation with both feet (actually, since you're the one planning this hullabaloo, that's probably not too far from the truth!). But not everyone is as socially comfortable, whether it's because of their shy nature or because of something that has happened in their life to make them shun the limelight.

To make your shy relatives feel a little more at ease come reunion day, you can:

- Get them involved early. One of the best ways to make someone feel like they're not an outsider is to bring that person in. Ask her to be one of your all-important volunteers. That way, she's in on the festivities from the get-go and will be thinking more about the particulars of the party then her fear of it.

- Keep them busy. This is not to say you should overwhelm the person with a hundred tasks prior to the reunion, but asking him to make a few phone calls or send a few e-mails is a good way to keep him in on the plans and, therefore, less likely to feel uncomfortable.

- On reunion day, give them a task. You can't do everything yourself anyway. By giving the person a job—putting her in charge of having everyone write in the sign-in book, organizing one of the family games, or helping with the food—she will not only feel needed and important, but doing something is also an ice-breaker.

If you've made sincere, gentle efforts with your family wallflower but the response has been less than enthusiastic, don't force the issue. You may think you're being extra welcoming, but it may be perceived as overbearing and alienating. He or she may need a little time to get comfortable with the idea of the reunion, or else simply isn't interested.

Love Me, Love My Family?

You may think your family is a hoot to be around, but your spouse or partner may consider a long day in the hot sun listening to Aunt Agnes talk about her bunions yet again a form of spousal abuse.

While you can't force your significant other to love your family the way you do, there are a few things you can do to make the reunion a little more bearable:

- Don't force your spouse to do anything he doesn't want to do. It's a sure-fire way to start off the party on the wrong foot for both of you, thus alienating your partner from the one person he may actually *want* to talk to during the reunion—you. You may think forcing your partner into participating in an activity will get him involved, but it may well backfire.

- Get your spouse involved in an activity you know she enjoys. Whether it's heading up the barbeque, organizing the potato-sack race, or designing the T-shirts, give her an activity that she likes and that allows her to feel a part of the day because of a special interest or talent she possesses.

- Keep the strolls down memory lane to a minimum in your spouse's presence. He wasn't around for this stuff, and although an entertaining story or two about the time you set Uncle Rudolph's rain barrel on fire when you were 12 is a fun glimpse into your past, it's a past that doesn't include your spouse. This is also a day for making *new* memories—ones in which your spouse will play a part.

Clan Clues

If your spouse generally prefers a good book to socializing, see if he or she would like to help you put together your family tree. Genealogy research is not only a fascinating activity, but it can also make your spouse feel more a part of your clan by learning about their history. (There's more about this in Chapter 12, "Shaking the Family Tree.")

A Few Tactics to Keep the Peace

Of course, you can't be expected to patrol the reunion with a whistle around your neck, policing the family to prevent mishaps and eruptions. But there are a few tactics you can employ to head off any uncomfortable moments:

- Separate the guests who don't get along. If you know that the minute Aunt Gertrude and your brother get in a room together all hell breaks loose, steer them toward separate activities. And for heaven's sake, don't seat them together!

- Change the scenery. If you see a slugfest brewing, ask one of the bickerers to help you with something to nip the confrontation in the bud.

- Designate family topic-changers. If you have a few family members who are particularly skilled in the art of conversation, solicit their help in heading off trouble. Ask them to steer any volatile moments back toward calmer waters with a little change of conversation.

While there's no guarantee that everyone will be on their best behavior, a little extra awareness on your part might help head off trouble before it starts. If not, though, whatever you do, don't blame yourself. You can't control every sticky situation, and you shouldn't expect yourself to.

The Least You Need to Know

- Don't exclude the so-called family black sheep—reunions are a time to come together, not stay apart.
- Get shy family members involved early on to make them feel they're on the inside instead of the outside looking in.
- Don't alienate your spouse with endless family nostalgia. Instead, concentrate on making new family memories that include him or her.
- Although you can't control other people's behavior, there are some things you can do to head off squabbles and keep the peace at your reunion.

Chapter

7

A Question of Congregation

In This Chapter

- Figure out what space will best suit your reunion needs
- Assess the benefits of renting a hotel, catering hall, or restaurant
- Exploring other indoor options
- Considerations for having an outdoor reunion
- Finding the most accommodating accommodations

In Chapter 1, "A Reunion by Any Other Name," we looked at the different types of reunions and space needs you'll require for them. For a backyard bonanza at your home or the home of a relative, the parameters are pretty clear: Limited space means a limited guest list. Clearly, if you're having a small reunion, a party at your place is the best choice.

But what if you're planning on a larger loop-da-loop with your lineage? You're going to have to think big. In this chapter, I'll help you figure out which of these options—hotels, restaurants, catering halls, parks, campgrounds, and so on—will best suit your reunion needs, as well as some tips for accommodating your overnight guests.

Gimme Shelter

By this point, you know that for a large or weekend-long reunion a backyard party is pretty much out of the question. You need to think bigger. You need a facility that will provide you with ample space, seating, and facilities suitable for larger crowds—that is to say, hotels, motels, conference centers, and catering halls.

Say Uncle!

You may think you have oodles of time to iron out the details concerning your site, but don't hold off. You are competing with other reunions, wedding receptions, conferences, and other events for the same space. Make sure you investigate your options and book early.

Of course, you may assume that because indoor facilities like hotels, motels, and catering halls are multipurpose dwellings they can supply everything you need, but remember what Grandma Gloria said about making assumptions. Make sure you ask some questions, such as the following:

- Does the price quoted for the space only cover the space, or are other items included (such as food, gratuities, and taxes)?

- How much is the deposit and when is it due?

- Is there an installment plan offered to pay the balance, or is all the cash due on reunion day or earlier?

- If food is not provided by the site, is there a kitchen facility that you or a caterer can use?

- Are soft drinks and liquor provided?

- Is service (waiters, bartenders, servers) provided?

- How many people does the space hold? You may have figured that your reunion is going to be for 150, but does the site in question hold that many guests *and* allow for comfortable seating and table space?

- How long will you have the site or room? Will there be a party before or after yours? This might not seem to be an item of concern for you, but if you find you're being hustled out of the room you rented at 10 o'clock on the dot and there's no option to keep the party going, you'll be sorry you didn't ask.

- Is there a parking facility? Is it included in the price?

- Is there a place to hang coats or a coat check? If so, is there an extra charge for this?
- Will there be someone on hand during the party just in case something goes wrong or you have questions?
- If you will be having music, are there noise restrictions? (In a hotel or motel, this might be a concern.)
- Is there liability insurance? In other words, if your accident-prone Aunt Agnes slips and falls, will you or the site be held liable?
- What's the cancellation policy?

Many hotels and motels charge more during what they consider prime times; that is, the high season in the area. For example, prime time for hotels near major amusement parks might be during the summer or spring break when the kids are out of school. Also, prices tend to be higher for Saturday soirees as opposed to a Friday or a Sunday. If it's amenable to your family members, consider having the reunion on an "off" time to save on costs.

And remember the most important thing to do when booking a facility: *Get it in writing!*

Other Indoor Options

When your funds or the facility options in your area are limited, you need to get a little more creative. Think out of the hall, if you will. There's more than one place to hold a party. Consider any of the following ideas if the hotel or catering hall options you're finding aren't fitting into your plan or budget:

- Local clubs (Lions, VFW, etc.)
- Schools
- Religious retreat centers
- Indoor park facilities (picnic houses, conference centers, etc.)
- Galleries
- Museums
- Marinas (some will rent out their boat storage facilities during the warmer months when seafaring vessels are out of storage)
- Vineyards (most have indoor facilities that they rent out for special events and occasions)

 Clan Clues

For more site ideas, call your local chamber of commerce or tourism board. Also, don't overlook local real estate agents—they may know of people who rent out their homes for parties and other occasions.

The Great Outdoors

Holding your reunion in wide open spaces where the family can enjoy the sunshine and beauty of the outdoors is a popular choice for clan gatherings. The scenery becomes as much a part of the memories as the communal spirit engendered by bringing everyone together.

You have a few options for outdoor sites: public parks (from the small neighborhood park to larger, state-run park sites); the beach; and campgrounds.

 Family Jewels _____

> Nature doesn't move in a straight line, and as part of nature, neither do we.
> —Gloria Steinem, *Revolution from Within* (1993)

For parks and campgrounds, you'll likely have many of your reunion activities built right into the site: hiking trails; lakes or ponds for swimming, fishing, and canoeing; trail riding; local natural wonders; and the like. This is, of course, a great plus to holding an outdoor reunion. But make sure you keep the following important points in mind when considering the great outdoors:

- Check to see whether you need to get a permit to hold your gathering. These are generally just a formality and not difficult to secure, but secure them you must.

- Find out whether you are permitted to cook on the grounds or beach area. If you're planning on setting up the portable grill and a park ranger comes along and tells you it's not allowed, you'll all be left munching on hot dog and hamburger rolls.

- Ask if there are noise/decibel restrictions on music.

- Find out if alcohol is permitted.

- Find out if pets are permitted.

- Ask about restroom facilities (more on this later in the chapter). Are there adequate facilities, and how close are they to where you'll be having the party?

- Ask whether the grounds have their own insurance policy (if someone gets hurt, who pays the bill?).

- If you're looking into campgrounds, make sure they have dates available for when you want to hold your reunion (yes, you need to book a campground like any other site!)

- Plan to designate volunteers to keep an eye on the kids—the last thing you want are the wee ones wandering off into the wild.

- If there are natural bodies of water or a pool, find out whether there are lifeguards present.

- If there are lodging facilities on the grounds, find out whether there is a meal-plan option.

- Make sure you bring along a first-aid kit that includes Band-Aids, gauze, cotton balls, bandages, bug spray, tick repellent, hydrogen peroxide, antiseptic ointment, iodine,

and aspirin or pain reliever. Also, make sure
you know where the closest hospital is and
keep the number (and a fully charged cellu-
lar phone) on hand during the party. When
you're dealing with potential problems like
bee stings or heat stroke, it's smart to play it
safe.

 Clan Clues _____

> The YMCA has conference centers around
> the country that offer lodging, meals,
> campgrounds, and lots of outdoor activi-
> ties. Check out your local Yellow Pages for
> the YMCA conference center near you.

An Umbrella for All: Tents

If you're going with an outdoor site, you may want
to give serious consideration to renting a tent. As
I said earlier in this book, there's nothing like a
downpour or a case of sunstroke to put a damper
on the party.

You'd think there wouldn't be much to consider
with a big top, but there is. For instance, did you
know that not all tents are waterproof? This will be
fine for shelter from the UV rays on a sunny day,
but if it rains, your reunion will be a big, leaky
mess.

When renting a tent, be sure to find out the following from your vendor:

- Is the tent waterproof? If not, how much extra does it cost for a rainproof shelter?

- Does the vendor provide temperature control (heating and/or cooling systems)? If not, what's the extra cost for this?

- If something goes wrong with the tent during your reunion, will there be someone on call to fix any mishaps quickly?

- Is the tent open on all sides or does it have flaps to put down in case of inclement weather?

- Are there lighting fixtures or other options for when the sun goes down?

- When and how will the tent be set up and broken down?

Tents come in a variety of sizes and shapes, which all have different price tags. Make sure you get the price list from your vendor up front so there aren't any extra hidden charges to surprise you later on. Use the following table as a basic guide to judge how much tent you need. Keep in mind that if you plan on serving food under the tent you'll need more space, because the tables and chairs take up more room.

Square Feet	Number of Guests
200	15 to 30
400	30 to 65
450	65 to 100
800	100 to 150
1,350	150 to 200

If you can't find a tent rental vendor in your area, a good source is the American Rental Association (1-800-334-2177). They also supply other party essentials such as tables, chairs, and linens.

Skip to the Loo

If you're holding your reunion outside, don't fail to overlook one very important detail: bathroom facilities! If a port-o-potty is something you'll need to look into renting, keep the following in mind:

- Make sure they're set up close enough to the site so folks can get to them quickly, but far enough away so any, er, septic mishaps don't spoil the aroma of the day.

- Make sure they are stocked with plenty of toilet paper. The vendor may not provide more than a roll or two per potty (ask about this ahead of time!).

- Consider providing amenity baskets in your latrines. You don't have to get fancy, but a basket with safety pins, Kleenex, Band-Aids, a compact mirror, antiseptic ointment, bug spray, tampons, and premoistened towelettes might save the day for any personal mishaps suffered by one of your near and dear.

If there aren't any commode-ity brokers in your area, try calling Porta-John at 1-888-767-8256, or if you have access to the Internet, check out www.toilets.com or e-mail info@toilets.com.

Sleep on It

As you figure out where your reunion will be held, your family is going to need to think about where they can bunk if they're going to need to stay overnight. The following list of hotels can be found in most major cities and offer a variety of discounts:

- **Holiday Inn (1-800-HOLIDAY, 1-800-465-4329, or www.holidayinn.com).** In addition to offering group discounts, Holiday Inn offers free meals for kids under 12, 25-percent senior citizen discounts, a 30-percent discount off the price of a room if you book more than 21 days in advance, and their "Next Night Free" offer if you book for more than one night. Check out www.sixcontinentshotels.com/holiday-inn for more details or to book reservations online.

- **Marriott Hotels (1-800-228-9290 or www.marriott.com).** Marriott has locations all over the country and offers group discounts.

- **Hotel Locators (1-800-576-0003 or www.hotellocators.com).** This service allows you to speak with a group planner specialist, who will discuss your reunion's special requirements and help you find the best price available. Or you can fill out the online group planner form at their website.

- **Super 8 (1-800-854-9518 or www.super.com).** This popular motel chain offers special group discount rates and on-site amenities to make your stay more comfortable. They also have group meeting areas available.

The Least You Need to Know

- Don't wait to book your site—as soon as you have a head count, secure your reunion spot.

- Don't assume that once you book everything will be done for you. As pertinent questions, make sure you know what's included with the facility, and get it all in writing.

- Consider other indoor options such as schools and museums if your funds are tight or if the number of hotels or restaurants in your area is limited.

- When holding a reunion outside, don't overlook the need for a tent or other shelter as well as bathroom facilities.

- Lots of hotels and motels offer group discounts, but you have to ask!

All Together Now

In This Chapter

- Save your sanity: delegate!
- Create committees to get the jobs done
- Matching the task to the personality
- Lining up help on reunion day
- Working together doing the little things makes for big memories

Remember back in school when you had a big exam to study for and the amount of information seemed so overwhelming, you had no idea how you'd plow through it all? And then you discovered something: the study group. You got together with a few trusted friends, and together you tackled that seemingly insurmountable mountain of information and made it into a much less formidable molehill.

Hmmm ... not such a bad idea for reunions either, is it?

When you embark on planning your reunion, the challenges ahead of you—tracking down family members, setting a date everyone can agree on, renting a space, getting the food, and the 1,001 other details and to-dos—might make you wish you were an orphan. But there's a simple solution to your overwhelming overload of odd jobs: delegation. In this chapter, I'll show you how lining up a few trusty sidekicks will help you get the work done without losing your enthusiasm for your lineage.

Don't Hesitate to Delegate!

Believe it or not, there's an art to delegation. It's not just about being a bossy, take-charge kind of person or, on the flip side, being too lazy to perform the tasks at hand yourself. If this is what you think about when you hear the word *delegate*, erase those thoughts from your mind immediately. Everyone needs a little help sometimes—and when you're undertaking the monumental task of planning a reunion, you're going to need a lot of it. So get over any delegation hesitation you may have had in the past and learn this now: You will not be able to get through this with all your senses intact if you don't solicit some help.

With this in mind, let's start out with a few rules of thumb for rounding up help:

- Ask! Don't just wait for family members to step up to the plate—make requests for help. There may be several ready, willing, and able volunteers at your disposal, but they just don't realize you need assistance. Don't be shy about requesting aid.

- Assign jobs according to talents and interests. If you do this, your volunteers are more likely to get the tasks done and done well.

- Choose the reliable, not just the enthusiastic. Enthusiasm is a great quality, but if you know that your Cousin Chloe is notorious for thinking big but not finishing strong, don't give her a large project that requires serious amounts of self-motivation. Instead, use her enthusiasm for projects that she can do with you: making out the invitations, sorting through the filled-out questionnaires, or helping you cook. This way, that go-get-'em attitude is directed toward projects where you can make sure it's put to good use.

Say Uncle!

Don't make yourself a martyr. The "it will only get done right if I do it myself" attitude will not only stretch your personal resources as thin as the hair left on Uncle Harold's head, it will also likely cause mistakes and problems along the way.

You can divide your volunteers into three different categories:

- Independent volunteers
- Isolated-task volunteers
- Reunion-day volunteers

Let's look at each of these volunteer types to help you figure out what (and how much) they can do for you.

Categorically Committed

While all helpers will be integral to pulling off a successful reunion, independent volunteers are your secret weapons. These are the folks who are equally as committed to the task at hand as you, are responsible and independent enough to take on a larger project, and don't require a lot of supervision.

With this type of helper, you should take full advantage of their independence and reliability. Establishing committees that your independent volunteers head up is an excellent way to do this. It gives them a greater sense of commitment and involvement in the reunion.

 Family Jewels _____

> I don't keep a dog and bark myself.
> —Elizabeth I (ca. 1590)

Committees can be created for any task, depending on the size and type of your reunion, but some of the more useful groups might include the following:

- Tracking down relatives who you'd like to invite to the reunion
- Researching the family genealogy
- Raising funds
- Researching possible reunion sites
- Handling the food (planning the menu, soliciting and organizing family recipes, finding and working with a caterer, etc.)
- Checking out accommodations and transportation options
- Handling photography
- Organizing favors/giveaways
- Organizing games and entertainment
- Creating reunion handouts and information packets
- Organizing the set-up and clean-up
- Creating the family website

If you do decide to put a volunteer(s) independently in charge of a particular aspect of the reunion, make sure you have a check-in day each month where—either by phone or in person—your committee head(s) gives you a progress report on what he or she is doing and how it's coming along. As the chief organizer, it's important for you to keep track of all the details, and, if you or your volunteers are running into snags, you can put your heads together to find solutions.

Clan Clues

> Make sure you keep a detailed list of who's doing what. If you ask Cousin Fran to pick up the T-shirts, and then forget you requested this and ask Aunt Sally to do it, too, you're wasting precious time and energy redoing tasks.

Isolated-Task Helpers

Different personalities are suited to different tasks. Just because some of your volunteers function well without supervision doesn't mean that those who need a watchful eye aren't going to be just as vital to your well-oiled reunion machine. Or you may have some kids who want to help, but who aren't old enough to be put in charge of a task.

With these folks, organize tasks that you can do together. That way, you can provide instructions and structure, be there to answer questions, and get the job done right without having to do it all yourself. Isolated-task volunteers are well suited for …

- **Mailers.** Whether it's stuffing envelopes or addressing them, this task will get done a lot more quickly with some extra hands—plus it's the kind of thing you can all sit around a table and do together.

- **Cooking.** Get a volunteer or two to come over and help you get your end of the meal together (if you're planning on cooking for the reunion, that is). Whether it's washing vegetables, chopping, mixing ingredients, or making a marinade, this is not only a great help to you, but a fun thing to do together. One caveat: Plan ahead. Make sure you know what you want done before your volunteers show up, otherwise they'll end up watching you do your best imitation of Julia Child. Remember: These volunteers need direction and you have to provide it.

- **Shopping.** Divide up your shopping list into several smaller lists: food, paper goods, beverages, etc. Gather up your volunteers, give them their assigned lists, and go out for a day of shopping.

- **Sorting through family questionnaires.** This is a bigger task than you might think. Inviting people to sort through the family questionnaires will help you parse out and more easily record the information in your Reunion Notebook.

Don't forget to thank your volunteers! Just before the reunion or after it's all over, take your volunteers out or invite them to your home for a celebratory brunch, lunch, or dinner, if they live near you (if they don't, send them each a token of your appreciation). After all, you couldn't have done it without them—make sure they know that!

Rally 'Em Up for Reunion Day

You may think that everything will be done and you can wake up on the day of the party with nothing left to do, but that's simply not the case. You are going to need help on the day of the event, so don't forget to solicit volunteers to do the following:

- Set up the tables, chairs, food, etc. if you're having the party at your home or for a day-long larger event that isn't being professionally catered.

- Greet and direct guests as they arrive.

- Act as family referees (that is, help you head off any potential family squabbles by providing distractions). See Chapter 6, "Problem Children," for more on this topic.

- Make sure all handouts such as goodie bags, flyers, and T-shirts arrive at the reunion site and are given out to attending family members.

- Entertain and organize the activities for little ones (as well as keep an eye on them in outdoor situations).

- Run any last-minute errands that need to get done.

Clan Clues

Before paying for a service, make sure it's not something that could be done by a volunteer. Ask volunteers to write down their special talents or abilities, and record these in your Reunion Notebook. As tasks or needs arise, check your volunteer list to see if you can farm out the duty in question to someone in the family instead of paying for the service.

The Family That Works Together Stays Together

The final, and most important, benefit to gathering family volunteers to help you bring the reunion plans to fruition is one that will last long past the party. There's nothing like working on projects together to make new memories and bring you closer as a clan. Not only will you share in the joy of putting together an important family event, you'll also learn things about each other you may not have known, such as the special talents that each of you possess. Although you will remember your reunion for years to come, you'll also have the added benefit of the memories you made putting it all together as a family.

The Least You Need to Know

- Don't be shy about delegation. Planning a reunion is a large task, and one that requires the assistance of a few good volunteers.

- Assign your volunteers tasks that complement their abilities.

- To keep the more complicated facets of the reunion organized, create committees for your volunteers to head up.

- Enlist help for smaller (but important!) tasks for your volunteers who are enthusiastic but who do better with a little supervision.

- The biggest benefit to working together is in the shared memories you'll have.

Chapter 9

Dig In!

In This Chapter

- Help in the kitchen—don't try to do it all yourself!
- Tips for incorporating cooking into the reunion
- How even weekend-long reunions can feature family cooking
- Tips for hiring a caterer

When it comes to food, there's one cardinal rule: There'd better be plenty of it. The last thing you want to do is turn folks away hungry (especially family—you know how grumpy Grampa Gus gets when he's not fed). But how do you plan to feed your hungry familial troops?

By now in this little book, you have likely sturdily settled upon how big your reunion is going to be. You may even have all your RSVPs back and are busily humming along in reunion-planning land.

In this chapter, we're going to hunker down at the family table and talk turkey (and mashed potatoes and cole slaw and peach cobbler and …).

No One Cooks Like Dear Ol' Ma

If you plan on firing up the barbeque or baking a batch of pies, more power to you. There's nothing like homemade anything—except, of course, the exhaustion that goes along with it. First and foremost advice for doing your own catering: Don't do it all by yourself! You are going to need help. Period. Even Martha Stewart herself has an ample staff to do all those exhausting home cooking and repair projects. (That's why she always looks so good for the photos!)

Ask relatives for assistance. Chances are they'll be more than happy (and flattered to be asked) to contribute their famous ambrosia surprise. But adhere to a few rules when asking:

- Get your requests in early. Once you decide on a date and guest list, figure out the basic menu you'd like to serve and get your assistant cooks lined up.

- Figure out how much you'll need. A good rule of thumb for food is a half-pound per person. So 10 pounds of potato salad will provide one serving for 18 to 20 people as a side dish, give or take. (Of course, you'll want to double that amount so seconds are an option. And if you've got big eaters in your family or are counting on leftovers, allow for slightly more, especially on main dishes.)

- Follow up on your helpers. Just because Aunt Thelma said "Sure!" doesn't mean she didn't get busy the week before the reunion and forget all about that fried chicken she was going to bring. A gentle reminder the week prior to the reunion will save you and your guest cook frustration and embarrassment. (And hey, this is a great task to assign to your volunteers if you don't have the time to follow up!)

- Make sure you have the proper cooling or heating accoutrements such as ice-filled coolers or plug-in hot plates. Of course, it's easiest to serve picnic-like food that's fine at room temperature, but I'm betting you'll be serving more than just potato chips and carrot sticks at your party. If you're planning on hot or cold dishes, make sure there are sternos and ice aplenty.

And for the spatula-challenged members of your family, keep a separate list of extras that you're going to need. When the noncooking guests ask if they can bring something, break out that list. It'll cut down on the money and time you spend shopping. Here are some helpful items to ask your guests to pick up for you:

- Condiments (mustard, ketchup, hot sauce, etc.)

- Fresh fruit
- Snack foods (potato chips, pretzels, dips, etc.)
- Plastic wrap
- Aluminum foil
- Ziplock baggies (small and large)
- Tablecloths
- Extra card tables
- Extra chairs
- Coolers
- Ice
- Hot plates
- Paper napkins
- Disposable utensils
- Disposable plates
- Disposable cups (insulated to hold both cold and hot beverages)
- Extra soft drinks
- Extra beer, wine, or liquor (if you plan on serving alcohol)

As far as what *you're* going to cook, follow these commonsense rules and you'll get to reunion day with energy to spare:

- **Plan ahead.** Clearly, if you're assigning out dishes you're getting a jump on your plan. But don't forget about yourself. What's left to do? What does that mean for you? If the work left to be done is still too overwhelming, get back on the horn (or get your volunteers on the horn) and round up a few more cooks. (This is a great way to make shy relatives feel more involved *and* alleviate some of the pressure on your end.)

- **Keep lists.** Don't rely on your memory to get you through to reunion day, no matter how small your party. With all those details to keep track of you're bound to forget something. Write down what you're making, what ingredients you'll need, what can be prepared ahead of time, how long you'll need for each dish, and how much you need to make. Then (yes, you guessed it) put it in your Reunion Notebook!

Say Uncle!

Few of us would deny that a cold beer on a hot day is mighty fine, but if you serve alcohol at the party, make sure your guests are okay to drive home when the festivities are over. At larger gatherings you can designate "checkpoint" volunteers to make sure everyone is okay to get behind the wheel before they leave. If

- **Get the kids involved.** If you have teenagers or children old enough to follow directions and wield a wooden spoon, allow them to help out. Not only will it help you, but it will make them feel involved in the reunion and an important part of the family.

● **Relax.** Oh sure, you may be saying, that's easier said than done, but really—if you cook yourself into a frenzy you will not enjoy (or maybe even remember) much of your reunion. You're not just the torch carrier, you're part of the family. This party is just as much for you as anyone. So go back to the first tip in this list and make sure you *plan ahead!* That way, you'll ensure yourself some well-deserved time in an easy chair.

Say Uncle!

If you plan on barbecuing on a gas grill, don't forget to check the fuel tank. If you're out of gas on reunion day and can't find a replacement, you're going to get stuck with a whole lot of burgers and hot dogs in your freezer. In fact, get a backup tank while you're at it—just in case.

Kiss the Cooks

There are lots of fun ways to incorporate cooking into your family reunion. Here are two excellent suggestions that involve the whole clan in the spirit of good food and good fun.

Baker Family Bake-Off!

A great way to incorporate cooking into your family reunion—as well as create some entertainment—is to up the ante with a little competitive spirit. (Come on, you know Uncle Dave is dying to prove once and for all that his chili beats the pants off of Uncle Steve's.)

When you send out your invitation (for a small reunion) or your initial questionnaire (for a larger reunion), include a notice announcing the family cook-off and the rules for it (for example, whether there will be categories; whether they will need to bring their own cookware, utensils, ingredients, and so on; whether they will need to bring the dish ready-to-eat; and that they will need to bring the recipe to be included in the family cookbook).

Assign an impartial judge as taste-tester (perhaps an in-law or spouse who feels a little out of the loop). You can even award prizes such as first-, second-, and third-place ribbons or a basket of cooking goodies—as well as a special note in the family cookbook announcing the award-winning recipes.

Clan Clues

If you've created a family website for your reunion (see Chapter 4, "Untangling the Web"), post the winning recipes on the site after the reunion so everyone can enjoy the award-worthy dishes.

Aunt Mala's Kick-Butt Masala

Another great technique for getting the family involved in the cooking is to incorporate your ethnic traditions into the menu. This might take a little more legwork on your part and the part of your volunteers, but it's a mouthwatering way to add your family traditions into the mix (and mixing bowl).

As with the cook-off, when you send out your invitation (for a small reunion) or your initial questionnaire (for a larger reunion), let family members know that the food served will be recipes from your family's heritage and that you are soliciting volunteers to contribute recipes and make dishes to bring. Don't forget to ask guests to bring the recipe they plan on using so it can be added to the family cookbook.

Cooking for a Crowd: Divide and Conquer

If you're planning a large or weekend-long reunion and think cooperative family cooking is off-limits for you, hold on there. It's not impossible to incorporate cooking fun into your reunion activities. One instance in which this activity will work is if you select a camping weekend for your reunion.

Think about it: When you camp, you have to cook for yourselves anyway. If you make cooking part of your reunion activities you will …

- Get everyone involved in the fun and working together.
- Be able to add another dimension to your reunion memories.
- Distribute the labor and financial burden.

Remember, large or weekend-long reunions can have as many as 200 or so guests (of course, there's no rule that says 25 of you can't go camping—you are more than welcome to get creative within these structures). When you send out your second mailing (or via e-mail if this is an option for your clan), solicit volunteer families to head-up a meal or two (breakfast, lunch, or dinner for a particular day). This might sound a little overwhelming, but it's easy if you assign teams to do the cooking.

Clan Clues _____

> Why not organize a prereunion shopping trip to the local supermarket? Load your local cooking volunteers into the car and do your collective food shopping together. It's a great prereunion group activity that saves both time and money.

It's probably best to divide the meals into groups of 20 to 25. If you have 200 guests, you'll need 8 to 10 volunteer families to head up each meal per day. You should create a separate "cooks" list in your Reunion Notebook that clearly delineates, day by day, who's heading up which meal. Then, underneath the "cook" families' names, divide up your guest list so that each family gets 20 to 25 hungry mouths to feed. On the first day of your reunion weekend, distribute a notice with the assigned chefs to arriving family guests so they know which cook to kiss.

Family Jewels

After a good dinner, one can forgive anybody; even one's relations.
—Oscar Wilde (1854–1900), Irish poet and novelist

Time to Call the Caterer!

There's a lot to be said for having someone else sweat it out in the kitchen rather than you. Not that cooking isn't a satisfying, fun activity, but since you're doing *all* the planning, you might want to consider completely delegating this important aspect of your reunion (especially if you're having a large or weekend-long reunion).

If you decide that using a caterer is best for your reunion circumstances, use the following rules of thumb to help guide you:

- **Ask around.** If you don't have a caterer you've used previously and trust, ask your friends or relatives who live in the area where your reunion will be held for their recommendations. If you can't find a caterer that someone you know has used and liked, check with the local Chamber of Commerce. They may well be able to recommend a few places with solid reputations.

- **Talk turkey.** Don't just sign on the dotted line. View the caterer's menu, discuss the food and price options the caterer has to offer, and ask if they will make items off the menu (for example, traditional family recipes you would like included).

- **Check out the goods.** See if the caterer offers a tasting of their food (many do). If a restaurant would be doing the catering, go in for lunch or dinner to see what the food is like and how professional the staff is. Think of it as a trial run before you sign on with this merchant.

- **Get it in writing.** No matter how well known your caterer is, don't agree to anything verbally or with a handshake. It's not that your caterer is looking to necessarily pull one over on you, but busy people forget things. To avoid any reunion-day food fights, make sure that everything you have ordered and agreed upon is in writing in a contract that both you and the caterer have signed.

- **Get the lowdown on leftovers.** It may sound silly, but ask your caterer for his or her policy on leftovers. You may assume that you get to keep them, but that may not be the case. Find out ahead of time (and get it in writing).

- **Know what you're paying for.** Will your caterer charge you extra for providing silverware? Staff? Linens? These extra charges need to be discussed and agreed upon (again, in writing) ahead of time. You might not need hors d'oeuvres at your party, so why pay for them?

- **Pad the list.** When you give your caterer your guest list, add 10 to 20 extra people to the head count. Remember: It's worse to run out of food than to have a little extra left over.

- **Follow up.** A week or so before the party, call the caterer to make sure everything is on track and to nail down any last-minute details. Make sure you know what time the caterer is expected to arrive.

If traditional catering options in your area are limited or out of your price range, don't overlook other venues. For instance, many local pizza places make more than just pies, and will be glad to provide you with a hearty and affordable spread for your reunion. You may have to arrange for your own pick up, but it could be worth the cost.

The Least You Need to Know

- Make sure you're not the only one feeding all those hungry mouths—line up help in the kitchen ahead of time!

- For home-cooked reunions, add fun activities like a cook-off or an ethnic family spread to get everyone involved and to keep family food traditions alive.

- Large and weekend-long reunions aren't off-limits to home cooking, they just require a little more strategic planning and a lot more volunteers!

- When hiring a caterer, make sure you ask questions, get everything in writing, know exactly what you're paying for, and follow up before the party.

Chapter 10

Eat, Drink, and Be Family

In This Chapter

- Why food can be an important part of your family history
- Tracking down and deciphering those old family recipes
- Incorporate family recipes into your reunion by creating a family cookbook
- Tips for making your cookbook special

You could barely sit still as the station wagon pulled into the familiar driveway. As soon as it came to a complete stop, you'd unbuckle your seatbelt, fling open the door, and charge as fast as you could through Grandma's front door. The great smell of her famous Calabrese eggplant perpettis (or apple strudel or chicken tika masala—feel free to insert your favorite olfactory memory) would immediately tickle your nose. It was an aroma that, to this day, distinctly and perfectly defines one thing for you: family.

Smell and taste are powerful factors in memory. Think about it: The smell of fresh-cut grass brings thoughts of summer; the pungent odor of mothballs reminds us of unpacking sweaters for the cold days ahead; the tart taste of apple cider hints of the brisk days of autumn. It's the same with family: There are distinct aromas that rekindle happy feelings and warm memories of your clan. In all likelihood, food is probably one of the most powerful triggers of this kind.

In this chapter, I'll show you how you can incorporate your family's favorite dishes into your reunion—and into the fabric of your family's collective memories for all time.

Food for Thought

When we think about a family's history, we might think about old photos, trips from the Old World through Ellis Island, or how we were brought here against our will, but fought for freedom and independence from the bonds of slavery. We think about stories and lore (the latter will be discussed in more detail in Chapter 13, "Once Upon a Clan") that weave together the beautiful tapestry that is each family's story. But stories can be told in more than words—they can be told in taste, too.

Believe it or not, your family recipes say a lot about your history. The dishes passed down from generation to generation act as a map of where your clan came from, where they landed, and how they incorporated themselves into that geographical area. Whether it be southern Italy or the southern United States, what you cook says a lot about who you are and where you came from.

What better way to season your reunion day than with dishes distinctive to your family?

Gathering the Recipes

The biggest hurdle you'll have to get over here is tracking down the recipes. Just like gathering stories, recipes aren't always in a complete form. Some dishes have been in the family so long, that they may never have been written down. Or they were put down in the "pinch and dash" form with no real measurements.

This is where you and your family sleuths will have to do a little legwork. Obviously, before breaking out the pots and pans you'll have to collect the recipes. You can do this in the same way you began putting together your guest list:

- Ask relatives with whom you're in touch on a regular basis for any family recipes or memories of dishes they have.

- Cast the net a little farther out and request recipes (or the basic gist of a dish a family member remembers) in your family questionnaire.

Once you've collected these, divide them into two piles: (1) completed recipes and (2) incomplete recipes or memories of dishes.

Clan Clues

In your questionnaire, use a separate page for your family recipe/dish requests. That way, you can easily separate the pages and put them directly into your Reunion Notebook (in the food section you've made, of course) for easy access.

Hold on to those completed recipes (I'll show you what's in store for those later in this chapter). For the incompletes, you and your volunteers will need to do a little culinary investigation.

Filling in the Missing Ingredients

In the same way that customs and languages can begin to fade into the fabric of everyday life in the melting pot of America, so can family recipes. Reviving or reinventing them can be a wonderful way to uphold your family's unique traditions for future generations. (Just make sure you have the time and interest to track down your family's food history. If you have enough on your proverbial plate already, adding more might spoil the stew. The point of the reunion is to get everyone together. Don't bite off more than you can chew!)

For those recipes that are incomplete or just memories of a certain type of dish, why not try to fill in the holes of your family's culinary history? To do this, assign each of your volunteers one of the dishes in question to research. Here are some ideas that can help you fill in the missing ingredients:

- Contact the family member who provided the dish and ask a few questions. What does she remember about it? What did it smell like? Was there anything distinctive about its odor or taste that she can recount? Any particulars she can recall—smell, taste, an ingredient—will be useful information.

- Crack open the cookbooks. There's a cook-book for every type of cuisine and cooking under the sun. Whether it be ethnic, re-gional, or otherwise, check out your local library or peruse the cookbook section of your area bookstore for more clues on the incomplete recipes. Can you find a recipe that sounds similar? If so, pay close atten-tion to the ingredients. This is where you may find your missing link.

- Fire up the stove. Take the clues you've gathered and try to piece them together. Of course, the only way to do this is to experi-ment with the dish. You and your volunteers can, of course, do this separately on your own time. However, if you can schedule a "cook-off" day, that makes the results of your collective research all the more fun. Plus, you'll have the benefit of several other budding chefs to help you adjust what's off about each recipe.

Again, before you embark on your family recipe research, make sure you and your volunteers have the time to do it. If you *can* fit it in to your busy schedules, the result will be the discovery of a missing family link or two that you've managed to preserve for future generations!

 Clan Clues _____

> A great source for recipes is the website Epicurious (www.epicurious.com). They have a database of thousands of recipes and culinary terms that may help you discover the secret ingredient to your elusive edible.

Melting Pot of Memories

In Chapter 9, "Dig In!" I talked about incorporating family food traditions into your reunion by including dishes from family recipes. However, there's another way to do this that will make a great keepsake for your clan: a family cookbook.

After you've gone through all the work of collecting and testing your family recipes, why not preserve them as you would any other family heirloom? A family cookbook can be as simple as photocopying and stapling together your collected recipes to hand out at the reunion. Or you can go one step farther and have them specially printed.

Family Jewels

One cannot think well, love well, sleep well, if one has not dined well.

—Virginia Woolf, author

If you've collected enough recipes, treat your family cookbook like any other by dividing it into sections (appetizers, main dishes, side dishes, beverages, desserts). Here are some ideas to make it even more special:

- Add a quote from the contributor of the recipe (his or her memory of the dish or an anecdote about why it's special). If possible, include the contributor's picture, too!

- If your family emigrated from and/or settled in a particular area of the world, include a map or photo of that area.

- Give your book a name. You can be as serious ("Farrah Family Food: A Collection of Cooking Throughout the Years") or silly ("Mixed Nuts: The Kooky Cooking Traditions of the Clark Clan") as you like.

- Have it spiral bound so it stays together and is easily used when cooking (spiral-bound books tend to stay open more easily and are a regular option at most printers).

- Use a clear plastic page to cover the front and back of the book or have the first and last pages laminated. That way, the pages are protected from tears and spills (and messy cooks!).

You might want to include a request in the family questionnaire for interested parties to put in an "order" for the book. That way, you'll know how many you'll need and won't run short or have an overabundance on reunion day.

 Clan Clues

> If you're paying out of your own pocket to print up copies, you may want to figure out what you've spent, divide it by the number of books you've had made, and sell the books at cost. That way, you don't get saddled with all the expenses.

A Map of the Senses

If many of your family's fondest memories seem to occur around a dining table, you should incorporate your family's food history into the reunion. It may be as simple as letting Uncle Pete slather steaks with his secret barbeque sauce or as involved as putting together and preserving your family's recipes. However you decide to do it, you'll be feeding both body and soul.

The Least You Need to Know

- Don't overlook your family's food traditions in your reunion—these memories can be just as important and potent as the photos in your family album.

- Tracking down family recipes may take some extra legwork. Make sure you have the time and resources before embarking on a culinary tour of the past.

- A family cookbook preserves your family's food traditions for the future and is a wonderful way to make these traditions a part of the reunion.

- Your cookbook can be as simple as a stapled set of pages, or go one step farther and include quotes, pictures, and other special touches.

11

Fun for the Whole Family

In This Chapter

- You're all together—now what?
- Fun in the sun: outdoor games
- Indoor fun for everyone
- Just for kids

You may think games are for kids (and if there will be children at your reunion, all the more reason to have them), but games do more than just occupy the wee ones. Games break the ice, warm us up, bring us together, give us team spirit, help us get to know each other better, and provide a laugh or two when we're feeling shy.

In families, we sometimes take for granted that we know each other so well, there's nothing more to learn—but you may be surprised at all the little quirks, talents, and bits of information you *don't* know about each other. All the more reason to have some planned activities for your reunion. In this chapter, you'll learn about some great games and activities to keep your clan entertained—and who knows, you might even learn something new about each other in the process!

Fun in the Sun

Of course, being outside on a gorgeous day is never boring. After all, nature provides its own veritable playground. That doesn't mean you shouldn't organize a few activities, though; especially if your reunion is going to be predominantly outdoors. Why? It's just too easy for everyone to fall into familiar patterns: Aunt Josie and Aunt Emma sitting together and gossiping like they always do; Uncle Al and your dad talking sports; Cousins Jennifer and Ally cliquing off into their own private conversations.

Say Uncle!

Don't forget to bring plenty of extra sunscreen to your outdoors reunion. It's the one thing that everyone forgets to bring—and the one item they most regret leaving behind!

This is not to say that there's anything wrong with the relationships as they are. It's normal for some family members to gravitate toward each other in the same way that friends do. However, one of the goals of a family reunion is to learn about each other and maybe forge some new relationships with familiar faces. And engaging family members in fun and games is a great way to do it!

There's a reason some games just don't go away. Quite simply, they're classics. You may roll your eyes and think, "Oh come on. Who still does that stuff?" The point is not really the game, but that you're all playing it as a family: working together, competing, and in the end falling down laughing because your potato sack blew a hole and 75-year-old Aunt Thelma wound up winning the race. Here are some of the tried-and-true classics that have worked for many a family reunion (and will for yours, too!):

- **Three-legged race.** In teams of two, participants stand side-by-side and have their left and right legs, respectively, tied together. Then, the "three-legged" teams race against each other to the finish line (if they don't all fall down first, that is).

- **Potato-sack race.** If you don't have potato sacks handy, any kind of sack will do—even a king-size pillowcase. Participants put their legs inside a sack and try to hop to the finish line first.

  For the three-legged and potato sack races, don't make the courses too long. Fifteen to twenty feet is ample room to make the race a challenge without making it an Olympic feat to finish.

- **Tug of war.** Using a long rope, divide your group into equal-size teams. Whichever team pulls the other over to their side wins. To make it more challenging and fun, turn on the hose and aim it at the middle so the "losing" team gets doused (which, on a hot day, may not feel like such a bad thing!).

- **Egg toss.** In teams of two or more, give each team a half-dozen eggs uncooked. Team participants stand three feet apart, tossing the eggs to each other one at a time. Increase the tossing distance by having each participant take a step back after each successful toss. The team who has the most unbroken eggs in the end wins.

- **Where's my mummy?** In teams of two, one person is the wrapper, the other the "mummy." Using toilet paper, one team member has to wrap the other person from head to toe covering every area of the body except the eyes, mouth, and nose. The first to wrap 'em up wins.

- **Orange pass.** In teams of no less than five, the first person tucks an orange under his or her chin and attempts to pass it to the next person in line. The next person has to take the orange under his or her chin and pass it along in the same fashion. Hands cannot be used and if the orange is dropped, it has to go back to the first person to start again. The first team to successfully get the orange to the end of the line wins.

In addition to these classic family games, you can add others into the mix. Sporting events are a fun way to bring out a little healthy family competition, while getting everyone to enjoy the outdoors. Softball, golf, badminton, tennis, volleyball, and Frisbee are all great activities that can require teams of two or more.

Family Jewels

I don't have to be enemies with someone to be competitors with them.

—Jackie Joyner-Kersee, Olympic track and field gold medallist, *Are We Winning Yet?* (1991)

Indoors but Never Bored

Just because the party's inside doesn't mean that you should all sit around on your duffs. Being inside gives you all the more reason to organize activities that get your group up and participating. Take a look at the fun ideas for indoor games in the following sections.

Who Is It?

This is a great way to bring together the generations in your family. For this game, you'll need a Polaroid camera, a pen, and four packs of Polaroid film. Take a picture of your older relatives (or for very large reunions, 20 to 30 of your older guests—this equals about two packs of Polaroid film) as they arrive. Ask them to write down three interesting facts about themselves on the back of the photo.

Give one photo to a young member of your family (a child of reading age or teenager). Gather the family together and have each photo holder get the rest of the family to guess "Who is it?" by asking the questions from the facts on the back of the photos. If someone guesses who it is, you can arrange for them to win a small prize. A bag of goodies like candy or cookies works just fine.

Once the identity is revealed, take another picture of the elder and younger members of the family and have the younger one write three facts about himself or herself on the back of it. The older family member keeps this photo and the younger one keeps the original. The great thing about this game is that not only does the whole family learn something about the elder members of their family, but older folks learn about the younger ones, too.

Family Telephone

Remember the old game "telephone"? You know, one person whispers information into the ear of the person next to him and then that person passes on the information, and so on. Usually by the time you get to the last person in the group, the story has changed remarkably. You can play this game but with a fun, family twist to it: The tale told should be a true family story.

So let's say you know that Grandpa Jack came through Ellis Island with a wheel of cheese in his knapsack, but he was made to surrender it to immigration security because people weren't allowed to bring in food from other countries. Begin with this true family story and chances are by the end you'll have a whole new tall tale.

 Clan Clues _____

> Add an extra twist to the game by having two teams of telephone participants. Give each team five true tales. The team that gets closest to the truth the most times wins.

Be a Star: Karaoke

If you're not up on the latest craze sweeping urban and suburban nightlife alike, karaoke is when you get up and sing to the music of songs you all know and love. The easy part is that the lyrics are either projected in front of you on a screen or given to you on paper so you can't miss a beat.

For a family reunion, you can give all those budding songsters a chance to strut their stuff and maybe even break the ice with some of the shy family members who can't resist joining in the fun. Try to get a karaoke machine that has songs that span the generations so that no one feels left out, and encourage duets and "singing groups" to bring more family members closer together. Karaoke units can be rented for about $50 to $200 (depending on what area of the country your reunion will be held in). Call or visit your local electronics store to see if they rent them or can recommend a vendor who does.

Family Portraits

Have you ever been to a fair and seen an artist drawing portraits of people? Bring out your relative Rembrandt with a portrait-drawing contest. (This is another great way to match up the older and younger generations.) Ask for an equal number of volunteer models and artists and have the artists sketch their family portrait poser. Make sure you give them a time limit (20 minutes should be sufficient time for the "artist" to sketch and not too much time for the "model" to be sitting still). For this, you'll need to provide sketch paper, pencils, and erasers, and a prize for the best artist (a set of colored pencils or a sketch book make great gifts for this event).

Kids' Corner

Although the games and activities in this chapter are fun for the whole family, you still should provide some extra entertainment for the little ones in your clan. Try these ideas:

- **Arts and crafts.** Set up a table with crayons, colored pencils, paper, Elmer's glue,

Popsicle sticks, and other child-safe art materials for the kids to make their creations with. Be sure to bring in some old shirts for them to wear as smocks!

- **Face painting.** Using washable, skin-safe paint, have the teenage members of your group do face painting on the little ones.

- **Get-to-know-you treasure hunt.** Give kids an index card with a list of five questions to check off that are facts about a relative. The first to figure out who the person is wins.

- **Scavenger hunt.** Give kids a list of 5 to 10 items that they must collect from the guests (a penny, a stick of gum, etc.) or at the party (a pinecone, a flower, etc. if it's outdoors). The first to collect all the items on the list wins.

- **T-shirt making.** Little ones can make their own family reunion T-shirts using brushes and material paint. Again, have some old shirts on hand to protect their clothing.

One word of caution: No matter how free from danger an activity may seem, all children's games and events should be supervised by an adult or a responsible, older teenager. When it comes to kids, it's always better to be safe than sorry.

The Least You Need to Know

- Family games not only entertain, they break the ice and bring your family together.
- For outdoor games, don't overlook the good old classics.
- Just because you're indoors doesn't mean you have to leave the fun outside.
- Don't forget to plan some extra activities for the little ones.

Chapter 12

Shaking the Family Tree

In This Chapter

- What genealogy is and what it means to you
- How to get started tracing your roots
- Where oh where to look for your long-losts
- Incorporating your family tree into the reunion

When you begin planning a family reunion and thoroughly delve into the who, where, and what of your family, you can't help but wonder: Who *were* you before? The particulars of your family's history may have survived in bits and pieces of broken stories and fuzzy memories, but it doesn't have to be that way.

Engaging in research into your family's past is an investigative journey that can show you who your kin were, where they came from, and how you all ended up where you are now. More than that, though, discovering your family's history gives you all a gift of priceless and timeless proportions: your family's unique story. In this chapter, I'll show you how to climb the branches of your family tree and dig down deep to the roots to learn about your family's past.

Back to the Future

Let me begin by saying that genealogy research is no small undertaking. Once you uncover a few facts about your family's past, you'll be hooked. It's like starting with the first few pieces of a gigantic jigsaw puzzle: Once you start, you just can't give up until you can see the whole picture.

It's also an incredibly satisfying task. When you embark on filling in the gaps of your kin's past and begin to see clearly the picture of your family's unique history, it's almost as if you're hearing the voices of long-gone relatives telling you your family's stories.

 Clan Clues

Space doesn't permit me to give you more than just a few basics here, but if you want to learn more about genealogy, there are plenty of books on the subject. Also check Appendix A, "Web and Software Resources," for some great online resources to get you started on your genealogy research.

So what are you waiting for? Break out that Reunion Notebook and let's get started!

Tools You Can Use

Your Reunion Notebook will be an important part of keeping your search into the past organized—a key factor when you're trying to connect the disparate dots of the past. Create a separate genealogy section in your notebook in which you have the following:

- A page where you will begin to piece together the branches of your family (let's call this the "working family tree"). If you need to, you can make this a larger fold-out page by taping or stapling another sheet of paper to it.
- One sheet of paper for each nuclear family group (or "branch sheets").
- A page for recording the phone numbers, addresses, e-mail addresses, and websites of your sources for easy access.
- Pocket pages for holding various loose documents and important papers that you discover during your research.

You'll also need to use your home computer or, if you don't have one, get some time on one that has Internet access. Try your local library.

Starting Your Dig

Your working family tree sheet is where you will begin to piece together the branches of your family. At the top of the page in the center, write down the names of your grandparents. Underneath their names, record the names of their children (your mother/father, aunts, and/or uncles). Underneath your parents and aunts and uncles, write the names of their children (you and your cousins), and so on until you have recorded the basic nucleus of your family.

 Clan Clues

> To avoid writer's cramp, use the following standard genealogical abbreviations:
>
> b. = born   bap. = baptized
>
> m. = married   c. = circa
>
> d. = died   NMI = no middle initial
>
> bd. = buried   nd = no date given

For each of these "levels" you will create branch sheets to fill out the information about each family. Your branch sheets could look something like this:

Husband (full legal name):

_____

Birthdate: _____   City, state: _____

Date of death: _____   City, state: _____

Occupation:

_____

Father's name:

_____

Mother's name:

_____

Other spouses:

_____

Children:

_____

_____

Wife (full legal name, including maiden name):

_____

Birthdate: _____ City, state: _____

Date of death: _____ City, state: _____

Occupation:

_____

Father's name:

_____

Mother's name:

_____

Other spouses:

_____

Children:

_____

_____

Marriage date: _____

Where married (city, state):

_____

Children (repeat this information for each child):

Name:

_____

M/F [Circle one]

Birthdate: _____ City, state: _____

Date of death: _____ City, state: _____

Spouse:

_____

Occupation:

_____

Children:

_____

_____

You can also add to these sheets other pertinent, useful information, such as approximate dates for other big events such as graduations, moves, etc.

Once you get these basic facts down on your branch sheets—grandparents, aunts, uncles, and cousins—the holes you need to fill in will start to become apparent. Who were your great-grandparents? Maybe your great-grandmother's first husband died early in the marriage and she remarried. If so, who was her first husband and where did he come from? Were there any children from that first marriage?

Say Uncle!

Don't forget to record nicknames and changed names. They can be important clues in tracing your family's past. For example, your great-grandfather's real name may have been Edward, but everyone knew him as Buzzy. When researching him, you might find more facts under his nickname than his given one.

As you can see, the important questions about the past will begin to surface as soon as you start recording the facts you already know. But how do you fill in those holes of family information? Break out your Indiana Jones hat, friends, it's time to dig deeper.

Who Holds the Key to *Your* Past?

To fill in those elusive branches on your family tree, you're going to have to do some research. How much is up to you, your timeframe, and how much help you have in your family archaeological dig. Where to begin, you ask? You may be pleasantly surprised at the abundance of resources right under your nose (or a mouse click or field trip away).

Family Questionnaires

Begin fleshing out your family's past with the family questionnaire sheets you asked members to fill out early in your reunion planning. (Hopefully, you ensured a good response because you included those self-addressed, stamped envelopes!) Once you have all the useful information recorded on your family tree sheet, you may want to call some of your relatives to further dig into the information they provided. Ask ...

- How did they learn this information? Did they ever meet the relative(s) in question or was the information handed down to them from another family member? If so, who provided the information?

- Do they have any old photos of the relative? Are there other family members in the photos?

- Do they have any documents stored somewhere (such as old letters and correspondence, scrapbooks, yearbooks, journals, insurance papers, a family Bible, wedding or funeral sign-in books, diplomas, newspaper clippings, union cards, passports, Social Security cards, or report cards) that could provide more clues to the past?

You might feel a little shy about asking for this information, but think of the alternative: If you don't, your family's history might end up being lost to the past. That dusty trunk in your aunt's attic may seem like old junk to her, but it could provide a treasure trove of family information. Ask about it! Remember to take all the pertinent information you gather and add it to your individual branch sheets, and then fill in the missing links on your working family tree.

Family Jewels

Heredity: the thing a child gets from the *other* side of the family.

—Marcelene Cox, *Ladies' Home Journal* (1946)

This Will Go Down on Your Permanent Record

Excellent resources to your family's past are the permanent records kept in local, state, and federal offices, as well as religious institutions and newspapers. Documents you can use in your research include the following:

- Adoption records
- Automobile insurance papers
- Baptism records
- Birth certificates
- Charitable donation records
- Citizenship papers (immigration and naturalization documents)
- Death certificates

- Deeds
- Divorce papers
- Draft cards, military discharges, and military awards
- Driver's licenses
- School graduation records
- Income tax records
- Obituaries
- Wedding announcements
- Wills

In addition, there's the one major source of family information that you may want to look into: the National Archives and Records Administration (NARA). This federal organization's main branch is located in Washington, D.C., and has paper and microfilm resources for census records, immigration records, and immigration shipping and passenger lists, among many other useful bits of genealogy treasure.

If a trip to D.C. isn't within your grasp right now, you can request information about your family by contacting them:

> The National Archives and Records
> Administration
> 8601 Adelphi Road
> College Park, MD 20740-6001
> 301-713-6800
> inquire@nara.gov

If you write a letter or e-mail a request for information, be sure to include your first and last name, telephone number, mailing address, and fax and e-mail (if you have them) in the body of your letter so they can get the information back to you!

At the time this book was written, NARA was also working on an online searchable resource to use in your hunt for family history. Check their website at www.nara.gov.

Delving into all of these research techniques will take time (and likely, a little money), but these resources will prove invaluable to your finished product.

Telling Firsts from Seconds

Can't tell a first cousin from second, once removed? Here's a handy little cheatsheet to get to know who's who:

- **First cousin.** This is the son or daughter of your mother or father's sibling(s). This is also called a full cousin. You share a grandparent with your first cousins.

- **Second cousin.** This is the son or daughter of your parents' first cousins. You share a great-grandparent with your second cousins.

- **Third cousin.** This is the son or daughter of your parents' second cousins. You share a great-great-grandparent with your third cousins.

- **Once removed.** This refers to a cousin one generation removed; in other words, the children of your children of your cousins. So your second-cousin Sally's daughter Ann is your second cousin once removed.

Planting Your Tree on Reunion Day

You've dug and poked and scratched around for your family's history, and the result is a full, leafy family tree that you can be proud of. So now what? Put it away and let all your hard work go to waste? No way! This is not a project to be packed away—it's one to share with the whole clan.

For reunion day, print up or photocopy your final finished tree and distribute it to everyone at the reunion as a keepsake, or create on poster board a large-size version of your family tree and place it in a common area for everyone to see. Another idea is to have your reunion T-shirts printed with a picture of the family tree on the back. However you decide to display the fruits of your sleuthing labor, make sure you share it. This is your collective history—who you were, where you came from, and how you all got where you are now.

The Least You Need to Know

- Genealogy research is no small undertaking, but it's well worth the effort to learn about your family's history.

- Start with what you know about your family and branch out from there.

- Don't be shy about asking family members for help or more information. You're not prying—you're piecing together your history.

- Once you've filled in your family tree, be sure to share it with other relatives at the reunion!

Chapter 13

Once Upon a Clan

In This Chapter

- Why family lore is so important
- Old-world stories, establishment stories, and here-and-now stories
- How to incorporate your family's stories into the reunion
- Recording the tales for all to enjoy

As you've learned from the previous chapter in which you researched your family tree, every clan has its stories. From recent reminiscences of a fun family outing at the park to tales of Grandpa Joe's travels and trials in the New World, we all have our legends that we tell and retell to each other over the years. The oral tradition of storytelling has long kept families entertained, enthralled, and most important, in touch with their history as a clan. The problem with storytelling is that, as we grow and move, as generations pass on and new ones enter the world, the tales often get jumbled and, sadly, lost to the ever-accumulating years.

A family reunion is a wonderful time to accumulate your family's history, record it, and ensure that your stories don't get lost in the passage of time. In this chapter, I'll show you how to capture your family's tales—both old and new—and create your own collection of family lore.

Sleuthing Your Stories

Think of your family's saga as being like one of those three-part TV miniseries. You know how they work—part one establishes how it all started with stories of life in the "old country" and where the progenitors of the story came from; part two is the old generation establishing themselves in the New World and segueing into the next generation; part three is the story of the family in the present day.

With this in mind, you can divide your story gathering into this three-part saga:

1. Old-world stories—where your family came from and the ancestors who started it all

2. Establishment stories—how your family put down roots and grew in one part of the world

3. Here-and-now stories—what's going on in your family today

Let's look at each of these types of stories and how you, as the official recorder of family lore, can approach them.

Clan Clues _____

> You can use many of the same resources that I recommended in Chapter 12, "Shaking the Family Tree," to uncover your family's stories: newspaper clippings, old letters and correspondence, scrapbooks, yearbooks, journals, a family Bible, passports, and, of course, the elder members of your family.

Tales of the Old World

As you've learned, the act of tracking down and piecing together your family's history is like detective work. You're solving a mystery in that you're answering a set of questions: Where did your family come from? How did they get here? What motivated them to leave their homeland? Let's further explore these questions.

- **Your family's journey to the New World.** If your family emigrated from another country, where did they come from? Was it Europe? Africa? Or was it simply (well, maybe there was nothing simple about it!) a journey from one side of the country to the other? If you only have a vague idea of where your family originated, ask your existing older relatives to fill in the holes. If you do know where your family is from, see if you can find out more details, like the name of the city or town.

- **How your family arrived.** You might think this is an inconsequential detail, but stories of travel can be some of the most intriguing and fateful. Did your ancestors travel by ship? By covered wagon? Did they come through Ellis Island? Were they slaves brought here against their will? Did your great-grandparents meet during their journey to America?

- **Why they came.** It's likely that your ancestors had good reason to uproot themselves and start a whole new life in a new place. Why did yours? War? Famine? Work? To heal a broken heart? The hope for a better life? Try to glean the reasons your ancestors made the journey.

Say Uncle!

Tracking down ancestors who were brought to America as slaves is no easy task. Name changes, forced separation of family members, unrecorded deaths, and unmarked graves are just a few obstacles you'll encounter. An excellent resource is the African American Genealogical Society of Northern California. Write to them at PO Box 27485, Oakland, CA 94602-0985, or check out their website at www.aagsnc.org/index.htm.

Keep in mind when searching out your ancestral stories that they don't necessarily need to be tales of immigration. Maybe your whole family lives in California, but they began as Midwesterners. What motivated their journey west, or vice versa? Curiosity will be your greatest asset in seeking out your family's history.

Establishment Stories

Part two in your family saga are the stories of how your kin established roots in their home territory. What were your family's struggles in making a life for themselves? These tales can take the form of the following:

- **Assimilation stories.** How did your family ingrain themselves into their new homeland? Did they change a last name in order to make it sound more "American"? Did they involve themselves in community affairs? Were there other family members around to ease the transition, or were they completely on their own?

- **Struggle stories.** What hardships did your family have to overcome? How did these struggles change their everyday lives and, inevitably, their future?

- **Success stories.** What were your family's early triumphs? Did your great-grandfather start out as a grocery delivery boy and eventually work his way up to being the store owner? Did your grandmother's handmade quilts win her awards at the state fair?

Stories of the Here and Now

Lots of attention is paid to the past, and for good reason. Tales of struggle, hard times, and triumph over adverse conditions are full of the rich details that makes for an edge-of-your-seat saga. Interestingly, though, many folks pay less attention to the here and now. We tend to take the day-to-day events of our modern lives for granted. After all, compared with the struggles of your ancestors, life now can seem pretty darned boring.

Ah, but it's not. The good life you lead now is the result of the path chosen by your predecessors—and don't you think they'd be proud of where you all are and what you're doing? The birth of new family members, buying a new home, getting a college education, taking a major trip, celebrating a milestone anniversary—all of these events are part of your family's here and now and should be as carefully recorded as the tales of the past.

When recording your family history, find out what's going on with everyone at this moment. Fifty years from now, your daughter's granddaughter may learn something about her family that she wouldn't have known if that precious piece of information hadn't been recorded for posterity. You are making history right here, right now, just by planning this reunion. Think about the future generations and what they'll want to know about you and the rest of your clan today.

Clan Clues

The American Immigrant Wall of Honor in Ellis Island is a place where you can pay homage to your immigrant ancestors by having their names inscribed on the wall. If you're interested in commemorating your family's history this way, contact The American Immigrant Wall of Honor, The Statue of Liberty–Ellis Island Foundation, Inc., 52 Vanderbilt Avenue, New York, NY 10017-3898.

Reunion Time Is Story Time

Sure, gathering the troops for a big reunion is a great way to spend time together, but you, as torch carrier, have a hidden agenda: making a family storybook.

Think about this: How often do you have all of your family members together? Probably not very frequently. Take advantage of it! There's no better time to get the family storytelling going than when there's a captive audience. This is a great opportunity not just to entertain the troops and have the stories told, but also for them to be recorded and captured for the future.

During your reunion, set aside some storytelling time. You can do this in a spur-of-the-moment fashion, in which you gather everyone together and ask family members to recount stories of the past and present, or you might want to organize it. If you like, you can have a story sign-up sheet prominently displayed early on to get your clan members thinking about the tales they'd like to share. On the sheet, give them ideas as to the kinds of stories that would be great to hear (use the ideas I mentioned in the previous sections to help them along).

Then, during story time, make sure you capture the moment for the family history book. You can …

- Have one or two family members write down the story as it's told. Since they are going to be writing quickly, ask that they take a few moments after story time to embellish on the notes and add details they didn't have time to record. It's important they do this now because they'll have the advantage of having the storyteller there to answer questions.

- Tape-record the storytellers and later transcribe the story.

- Videotape the storytellers. You can transcribe the story later on for the family storybook, or you can create a family story video, which you can make copies of and distribute to family members after reunion day.

Family Jewels

Heirlooms we don't have in our family. But stories we've got.

—Rose Chernin, *In My Mother's House* (1983)

Choose whatever method is easiest and most practical for you. The point is to get those stories recorded for all time. This isn't just any old history, it's *your* history. And generations from now when the future members of your family are sitting around telling and retelling the tales of your collective clan, they won't just be entertaining each other, they'll be keeping alive important memories.

The Least You Need to Know

- Your lore isn't just ancient history—it's the story of how your clan became a family. Treat it as you would any precious family heirloom.

- Ask questions: Where did your family come from? How did they get here? What motivated them to leave their homeland? What struggles and triumphs did they experience?

- Don't forget about the here and now—someday it will be as much a part of your family lore as the story of Grandma's journey through Ellis Island.

- Invite family members to reminisce at the reunion, and make sure to record the stories for future generations to enjoy.

Chapter 14

Memories and Mementos

In This Chapter

- What's so great about mementos?
- Great ideas from T-shirts to trivets
- Personalize your mementos!
- Fun mementos you can create as part of the reunion
- The traveling family letter
- Piñatas and other kiddie fun

It's not likely that anyone in your clan will forget your reunion after it's over. The memories of the day or days you've spent together will be the thing stories are made of for years to come. Maybe you all had such a great time, you'll be planning the next reunion before the first one is even done. That is, of course, how it should be. You want to fire up that spirit of family closeness that is too easily lost in our busy lives.

What can you do to keep those warm memories alive long after your family reunion is over?

Providing all your reunion guests with a keepsake of the event is a great way to allow everyone to take a little piece of the day home with them. From T-shirts to a traveling family letter (you'll find out what that is in just a few pages!), there are many ways to provide your family members with a reminder of the fun you've all had. In this chapter, I'll talk about the different kinds of reunion mementos that will keep the family spirit in the air long after the reunion ends.

Great Mementos from A to Z

There are lots of fun, inexpensive memento ideas you can choose from. Some of the most popular are those that you can put on or carry. Wearable keepsakes are constant reminders of the fun you all had together. Some items you can use to stock up your family's collective wardrobe (and memories!) include the following:

- T-shirts
- Baseball caps or ski hats
- Tote bags
- Aprons
- Waist bags ("fanny packs")
- Bandannas or scarves

Aside from their wearability, the big plus of most wearable mementos is the space you have on them to print your design. Take full advantage of this! If you've created a family tree, for instance, you can use it as part of your design (it's also a great way to keep everyone in-the-know on your family's history). You can also use family photos as part of your design (just make sure that if you're using an old photo for which there is no negative, you stress to the vendor that it's irreplaceable!). Whatever design you decide to use, make sure you include the date of the reunion and (of course!) your family's name.

Most print shops will screen the design of your choice onto a T-shirt. However, you will probably have to provide them with a disk with the image on it. Check out Appendix A, "Web and Software Resources," for some reputable places that will provide you with designs and do all the work for you. (They also provide bulk discounts—the more you buy, the less you pay per item.)

Clan Clues

> If you plan on having another reunion, get a group shot of your clan at this year's party and have it printed up on T-shirts for next year's reunion!

If T-shirts and hats aren't up your family's alley, there are lots of other items that serve as great kin keepsakes. Consider any of these giveaways for your reunion (and don't forget to personalize them with your family's name and reunion date):

- Mugs
- Picture frames
- Trivets (also called hot plates)
- Blow-up beach balls
- Beach towels
- Frisbees
- Umbrellas
- Kites (also a great activity to engage in at the reunion!)
- Paper fans
- Plants or seeds (you can add personalized ribbons to these, personalized with the family name and reunion date)
- Pencils
- Tennis or golf balls (if your family participates in these sports)
- Magnets
- Matchbooks

 Say Uncle!

Beware of giving out knick-knacks that will just become dust collectors instead of fun family reminders. Try to keep an item's usefulness in mind when deciding on your party favor. If it can't be worn or used in some way, think twice about giving it to guests.

Also, don't forget about some of the things I've already discussed in this book. The family cookbook, family address book, and family history book all make wonderful keepsakes.

Make the Memento Part of the Party

If you want to make your keepsakes—and your reunion—that much more memorable, you may want to consider making the keepsake part of a family activity or game.

Family Jewels

I wear the key of memory, and can open every door in the house of my life.

—Amelia A. Barr, *All the Days of My Life* (1913)

How about having a family "grab bag"? You can gather your clan at some point during the reunion (toward the end of the event is probably the best time so guests don't lose track of their keepsakes during the day) and have them reach in and pick out a surprise favor. You can mix any of the previous ideas and put them in a large garbage bag, laundry bag, or pillowcase.

Another fun option is to do a "Secret Santa." You may be familiar with this from Christmas parties, but you can do it any time of the year. Assign each family member one relative (or have guests draw names) and have that relative buy a memento for that person. It's best to give a price limit (perhaps no more than $20 per gift) and provide guests with some ideas ahead of time to help them along.

If you don't have time to have items printed beforehand, you can have a family arts-and-crafts hour during the reunion. Provide guests with plain white T-shirts, mugs, aprons, hats, or whatever you like, and the appropriate paint and paintbrushes, and have them create their own reunion mementos that they can keep for themselves or create for other family members.

Create a Traveling Family Letter

One more idea you might want to incorporate is a traveling family letter. As you might glean from the name, it's the kind of favor that is created after the reunion is over. The traveling family letter is a great way to keep family members up to date on each other's lives and in touch with one another long after reunion day is over.

You (or one of your volunteers) will begin the letter. At the reunion, have a sign-up sheet for the letter, on which family members who wish to participate put down their names and current addresses. Begin the letter by writing a short wrap-up of reunion day, and then go on to say what you and your family have been up to since. Make sure you staple several blank sheets of paper to your original letter. Include a self-addressed, stamped envelope and a photocopied page of the list of family names and addresses, and send the letter to the first person on the list. That person adds to your update, and sends it on to the next person, and so on.

Not only are you all getting some welcome mail, but you're holding the family ties together, too!

Keepsakes for the Kiddies

Not all keepsakes are as desirable for kids, so you may want to consider having special favors made just for them. Consider any of these ideas for something the young ones will love to take home—and don't forget to have (or paint yourself) your family's name on them:

- Stickers
- Buttons
- Yo-yos
- Balls
- Candy

 Clan Clues

You can order candy with a special family message printed on the candy wrapper—see details in Appendix A.

You can also encompass some or all of these items into a fun event for the kids with a piñata. These can be ordered or, if you're feeling ambitious, you can make one yourself using papier-mâché. If you decide on the latter, what follows is the basic "recipe" for a fun family piñata. These simple instructions will result in a round, brightly colored piñata that you can decorate with your family name. (If you want to create a more complicated design, check out www.bry-backmanor.org/holidayfun/pinata.html or msms.essortment.com/howtomakepina_rgts.htm.)

You will need:

- One large balloon
- One large bowl
- Several sheets of newspaper to protect your work surface
- More newspaper cut into 2-inch-wide strips
- Papier-mâché paste: Boil 2 cups of water in a saucepan. In a bowl, combine $1/2$ cup all-purpose flour with 2 cups of cold water and add this to the boiling water. Bring the mixture to a boil, remove from heat, and stir in 3 tablespoons of sugar. Allow the mixture to cool, then place it in a bowl.
- String
- Scissors
- A knife
- A pin

- Different colored paints and a paintbrush
- Filling for the piñata (small toys, trinkets, candy)

Blow up your large balloon, knotting the end as you normally would. Dip the newspaper strips in the papier-mâché mixture, stripping off any excess using your middle and index fingers, and carefully place them across the balloon until the entire surface is covered and the outside is fairly thick and firm. Allow to dry overnight.

Once the piñata has dried, use the pin to pop the balloon inside. Paint and decorate the piñata any way you wish.

After paint has dried, carefully cut a three-sided square slightly off center at the top (this is the flap that you can open up and put the candy/toys into). In the center of the piñata, use the knife to poke two small holes about an inch and a half apart. Thread your string through the holes and fasten to a tree branch. Give the kiddies a broom handle or other sturdy stick for taking a whack at the piñata.

Although it's traditional to blindfold the person hitting the piñata, with small children you may want to forego this in the interest of safety. Even so, make sure everyone is out of harm's way from the hitter!

The Least You Need to Know

- Family favors are a great way to send your clan home with a reminder of the wonderful time they had at the reunion.

- Be creative in your choice of mementos, and make sure your family's name and the reunion date appear on it. You can also have a special design printed on keepsakes such as T-shirts or tote bags.

- Grab bags and "Secret Santa" gift exchanges are just two ways you can make mementos part of the reunion.

- A traveling family letter keeps everyone in the loop on family news (the best memento of all!).

- Special keepsakes just for the kids help get them into the family spirit.

Chapter 15

Preserving Those Memories on Film

In This Chapter

- Capturing the reunion on film keeps the memories alive
- Say cheese!: designating a family shutterbug
- Tips for hiring a pro
- Creating a family photo album

Memory is your mind's way of capturing all the little details of your life for you to revisit whenever you choose. It's your own little private screening room of the events that make up your life. But memory can at times be unreliable. The events of the past can take on a fuzzy edge, like an old photo that's slightly out of focus.

This is why the camera should be a key item at your reunion. Don't let all your hard work and the memories of your beautiful family get-together be left to your mind's eye only. In this chapter, we'll look at the different ways you can make sure your reunion is captured for all time on film and how to preserve those memories in special ways for the whole family to enjoy.

 Family Jewels _____

> One form of loneliness is to have a memory and no one to share it with.
> —Phyllis Rose, *Hers,* edited by Nancy R. Newhouse (1986)

Designating a Family Photographer

You and other members of your family will probably bring cameras to the reunion, so there will be *some* recording of the day's events. However, designating a family photographer will ensure that all the key moments—as well as all those little surprise, off-guard scenes—go down in your family's photographic history.

Who should you ask? But of course, I have some suggestions:

- **The shy guest.** A great way to involve those shy family members I spoke about in Chapter 6, "Problem Children," is to designate one as the family photographer. This gives him or her a vital role in the reunion-day activities.

- **The reluctant spouse.** Another figure from Chapter 6, the reluctant spouse, is an excellent choice for family photographer for a couple of reasons. First, if your spouse isn't so keen on strolling down memory lane, this gives him a job that's involving yet allows him to tactfully remove himself from conversations that may be (let's be honest) boring him to tears. Second, it designates this person in a vital family role, therefore including him in the day's events in an important way.

- **Teenagers.** Teenage family members some-times feel themselves stuck in a kind of family purgatory. They're too old to hang out with the little ones and participate in their games, but sometimes hanging around with the middle-age and older folks can be, well, *boring*. Designating a teenage guest as the family photographer gives her an important job that allows her to express her creativity (always an important outlet for teens) and gets her involved in the day.

 Clan Clues

There's no rule that says there has to be only one family photographer. You can ask a few family members to take on this task. This way, you'll get more than one person's perspective of the day. Or hand out disposable cameras to all of your guests at the beginning of the reunion and get everyone involved in the fun!

Once you figure out who the photographer is going to be, offer him or her a few rules of thumb:

- **Get group shots.** If possible, your photographer should try to get at least one large group shot. That way you can make copies and distribute the photo to all of your family members (a framed group photo makes an especially nice memento). If your reunion is so large that this might not be possible, several smaller group shots will do just fine.

- **Capture the off moments.** Some of the best (as well as most touching and important) moments are the ones when people aren't posing. Ask your family photographer to keep an eye out for the little moments that make for great memories.

- **Get shots of all the guests.** While it might be natural for someone to lean toward taking pictures of the family members he or she spends the most time with or knows best, make sure your family photographer gets shots of everyone. Otherwise, you may get a pile of photos capturing your Aunt Ida and Uncle Saul and not many of the rest of the clan.

- **Keep extra film on hand.** Give your family photographer a few rolls of extra film in an easy-to-carry bag. You don't want to miss out on capturing any great moments because he or she has to run back to the car or out to the store for more film.

- **Keep extra camera batteries on hand.**
  You'll want to check the camera's batteries
  before the reunion, of course, but keep an
  extra set on hand just in case.

Should You Hire a Pro?

If you have extra money in your reunion budget,
you may want to consider hiring a professional to
record the events of the day. Here are a few guide-
lines for going pro:

- **Ask around.** Just as you did with catering,
  ask friends and colleagues for the name of
  a photographer they've used and liked.
  There's nothing like a recommendation
  from someone you know.

- **Consider local universities as a resource.**
  Hiring a budding photographer still in
  school is an excellent way to have your day
  "professionally" captured for a whole lot less
  money. Check to see if your local college
  or university offers a photography major or
  courses and see if the administration can
  recommend a student or allow you to put up
  a flyer requesting one.

- **Check out the portfolio.** Make sure you
  like your photographer's style. If he or she
  likes to use lots of fancy effects but you just
  want a simple cataloguing of the day, that
  particular photographer may not be a good
  fit for your reunion.

- **Discuss what you want.** When you hire your photographer, make sure you discuss in detail what you want (and don't want); otherwise, you may end up with a pile of pink-tinted photos that don't do your great-aunt Edda's purple-tinged hair justice at all.

- **Be clear on the details.** Make sure your photographer is clear on the date, the time you would like him or her to arrive, and how long he or she is expected to stay (these details should be spelled out in your contract). Also, if there are particular shots you want taken, let the photographer know. Don't assume he or she will know what you want.

- **Find out *exactly* what the price includes.** When your photographer quotes you a price, make sure you know what this covers. You don't want to get a bill later on charging you for developing, extra film, overtime, or purchase of the negatives when you assumed it was included in the quoted price.

- **Learn the particulars.** Will you need to pay a deposit? How much? When is the full amount due? What's the cancellation/refund policy?

- **Get everything in writing!** I can't stress this enough. When you engage the services of a photographer, or any vendor, you *must* get all the terms of your agreement in writing. It's a simple way to protect both of you from misunderstandings or worse.

After you've gone over all of this information and signed your contract, make an extra copy of it and put it in your Reunion Notebook for quick reference.

Family Photo Album

Once you've had all of your film developed, don't just leave the pictures in their envelopes (stuffed in a drawer with all the rest of the photos you've been meaning to put in albums all these years!). Immediately put them in a special book that you've designated as the reunion family photo album.

This can be a simple photo album you buy at a store, or you can have an album specially printed with your family's name and the reunion date. An excellent resource for the latter is Exposures. This company offers many beautiful album styles and prints whatever you like on them. For a catalogue, write to Exposures, 1 Memory Lane, PO Box 3615, Oshkosh, WI 54901; call 1-800-222-4949. To see their offerings online, check their website at www.exposuresonline.com.

You can also create a virtual photo album online using any of the family website resources discussed in Chapter 4, "Untangling the Web." This is a great, less expensive alternative to having copies made that still allows everyone to enjoy the photos.

Clan Clues

PhotoWorks is a mail-order film-developing company that gives you the option of receiving electronic images online, on CD, or on high-quality paper. They also give you free film every time you develop a roll with them! Contact them at 1-800-746-8696, or check out www.photoworks.com.

The Least You Need to Know

- Capturing your reunion on film is the best way to ensure your memories last a lifetime!

- Designating a family photographer not only saves money, but gets family members more involved in the festivities.

- If you hire a professional photographer, make sure you know exactly what is included in the price and get it in writing.

- Once you get your photos, put them in an album you've designated for reunion photos so they don't get lost in the shuffle of un-catalogued pictures.

Web and Software Resources

From T-shirts to family trees, you'll find the following resources invaluable during your reunion planning!

Reunion Sites

Better Homes and Gardens
www.bhg.com
The magazine of home and hearth is also a wonderful online resource for family reunions. Covering topics like planning, genealogy, recipes for reunion day, and finding lodging and transportation for your family members, it's an excellent Internet resource. On the home page, type "family reunion" into their search option.

FamilyReunion.com
familyreunion.com
Although mostly a vehicle for vendors to hawk their reunion wares, this site does offer a live reunion chat session, a reunion announcing service,

as well as their "Reunion Poll," which allows family members to come to the site and contribute their ideas, information, suggestions, and plan preferences about their upcoming reunions.

Family-Reunion.com
family-reunion.com

(This is a different site than the preceding one; note the hyphen in the web address.) This website uses a character called Mr. Spiffy, the self-proclaimed family reunion doctor, to advise you on all aspects of planning a reunion. Sign up for their free newsletter or check out their message board and converse with other reunion planners. It was selected as one of the 101 best websites by *Family Tree* magazine in February 2000.

Gatherings: How Family Get-Togethers
Get Going
www.gatherings.info/index.html

This site offers tips, ideas, and information on food, entertaining the kids, games, spreading the word about your reunion, and capturing it on film.

Homespun Country Kitchen
homepages.rootsweb.com/~homespun/fr1.html

Here you'll find tips and ideas for family reunion planning, as well as links to other helpful sites.

Reunions magazine
www.reunionsmag.com

This website is your one-stop resource for everything concerning your reunion. There's a great search engine for reunion-friendly lodging nationwide, as well as links to other useful reunion-related sites. They're always looking for folks who have planned a reunion to contribute articles to their magazine, so you can become a renowned reunion author as well as the family torch carrier.

Mementos

A1 Candy Bar Wrappers
www.a1candybarwrappers.com
A1 offers candy bars in wrappers with personalized messages.

American Stitch and Print
www.american-stitch.com/noflashindex.htm
This company offers embroidered or printed designs (yours or theirs) on T-shirts, hats, bags, jackets, sweatshirts, sweaters, patches, pens, mousepads, and other items.

Graystone Graphics
www.graystone-graphics.com
T-shirts (long- and short-sleeved), sweatshirts, bandannas, aprons, hats, napkins, and tote bags are among the items that Graystone can personalize. You can provide your own design or use one of theirs.

Indian Lake Screen Printing
www.ilprinting.com/reunion.htm
This online company will print T-shirts with your own personal design or you can use one of theirs. T-shirts come in a whopping 17 different colors (some cost extra, though, so make sure you ask when ordering).

SweetNostalgia.com
www.sweetnostalgia.com
Although it doesn't offer personalized items, this
site features old-time penny candy that's sure to
bring a smile to the older members of your family.

Genealogy

FamilySearch.com
www.familysearch.org/Eng/default.asp
Created by the Church of the Latter-Day Saints,
this site allows you to search for relatives and share
your family history information, and gives useful
tips for genealogy research.

Genealogy Today
www.genealogytoday.com/home.html
This site has up-to-date news about genealogy,
family research tips, articles by regular columnists,
surname queries, and genealogy search tools.

MyTrees.com
www.mytrees.com
Check out this site for free searches for family sur-
names, Ellis Island searches, a Social Security death
index, and some access to Census information.

Genealogy Software

**Family Tree Maker, Deluxe Edition
(Broderbund), $69.99**
This fantastic, all-in-one genealogy software pack-
age allows you to keep your information (no matter

how nontraditional you may think your family is) organized and easily accessible, from names and dates to scanned photos, audio files (yup, you can record on this stuff), to a ton of other nifty little accoutrements. It creates family trees, maps, time-tables, and reports on your family's history that are not only easy to read and clear, but pretty darned nice to look at and present to the rest of the clan. It also gives you free access to Genealogy.com's exclusive search engine and data (which, without the software, you'd have to pay for separately).

Reunion Game

Family Reunion—The Game™—Where Every Picture Tells a Story (USAOPOLY)
Take the guessing out of what to do at your next family reunion. **Family Reunion—The Game™** is perfect for family reunions and any occasion where families and friends get together. Beautiful photographs take players on an extraordinary journey of storytelling fun when they learn about family traditions, share treasured memories, and reveal family secrets! Imagine learning about how your grandparents met or recalling some of your funniest childhood experiences. As players vie to collect photo cards for the win, *"You're Not Telling the Whole Story," Skeleton,* and *Family History* cards add just enough lively competition for any kind of fun-loving, crazy family. The winner assigns *Family Secrets* cards to all players, challenging them to reveal their best-kept secrets such as their first kiss

or a time they skipped school. ***Family Reunion— The Game***™ is housed in a beautiful keepsake box featuring a family tree to help players trace their own heritage. This game even comes with reproducible invitations so you can invite whomever you want for a special night of family fun. It's never the same game twice! Two to six individual players or teams. Ages 10 to grandparent. Call toll-free 1-888-876-7659 to find a retailer near you or call 1-888-656-7306 to order direct.

Appendix B

Recommended Reading

Browne, Ellen, ed. *Fodor's Complete Guide to America's National Parks: Official Visitor's Guide of the National Park Foundation, 11th edition.* Fodor's, 2001.

Burroughs, Tony. *Black Roots: A Beginner's Guide to Tracing the African American Family Tree.* Fireside, 2001.

Chrichton, Jennifer. *Family Reunion: Everything You Need to Know to Plan Unforgettable Get Togethers.* Workman Publishing, 1998.

Eichholz, Alice, ed. *Ancestry's Red Book: American State, County and Town Sources.* Ancestry Publishing, 1992.

Garten, Ina. *Barefoot Contessa Parties! Ideas and Recipes for Easy Parties That Are Really Fun.* Clarkson Potter, 2001.

McClure, Rhonda. *The Complete Idiot's Guide to Online Genealogy*. Alpha Books, 1999.

Ninkovich, Thomas, and Barbara E. Brown. *The Family Reunion Handbook*. Reunion Research, 1998.

Rose, Christine, and Kay German Ingalls. *The Complete Idiot's Guide to Genealogy*. Alpha Books, 1997.

Sachs, Patty, and Phyllis Cambria. *The Complete Idiot's Guide to Throwing a Great Party*. Alpha Books, 2000.

Sims, Betty. *Southern Scrumptious: How to Cater Your Own Party*. Scrumptious, Inc., 1999.

Stephenson, Lynda Rutledge. *The Complete Idiot's Guide to Writing Your Family History*. Alpha Books, 2000.

Wagner, Edith. *The Family Reunion Sourcebook*. NTC Publishing Group, 1999.

Index